MODES OF THINKING FOR QUALITATIVE DATA ANALYSIS

Modes of Thinking for Qualitative Data Analysis argues for engagement with the conceptual underpinnings of five prominent analytical strategies used by qualitative researchers: Categorical Thinking, Narrative Thinking, Dialectical Thinking, Poetical Thinking, and Diagrammatical Thinking. By presenting such disparate modes of research in the space of a single text, Freeman not only draws attention to the distinct methodological and theoretical contributions of each, she also establishes a platform for choosing among particular research strategies by virtue of their strengths and limitations. Experienced qualitative researchers, novices, and graduate students from many disciplines will gain new insight from the theory-practice relationship of analysis advanced in this text.

Melissa Freeman is Professor of Qualitative Research Methodologies in the College of Education at the University of Georgia.

MODES OF THINKING FOR QUALITATIVE DATA ANALYSIS

Melissa Freeman

Routledge
Taylor & Francis Group

NEW YORK AND LONDON

First published 2017
by Routledge
711 Third Avenue, New York, NY 10017

and by Routledge
2 Park Square, Milton Park, Abingdon, Oxon, OX14 4RN

Routledge is an imprint of the Taylor & Francis Group, an informa business

Library of Congress Cataloging in Publication Data
Names: Freeman, Melissa, author.
Title: Modes of thinking for qualitative data analysis / by Melissa Freeman.
Description: New York : Routledge, 2017.
Identifiers: LCCN 2016011088| ISBN 9781629581781 (hardback) |
ISBN 9781629581798 (pbk.)
Subjects: LCSH: Qualitative research. | Cognitive styles. | Thought and
thinking.
Classification: LCC H62 .F7225 2017 | DDC 001.4/2—dc23
LC record available at http://lccn.loc.gov/2016011088

ISBN: 978-1-62958-178-1 (hbk)
ISBN: 978-1-62958-179-8 (pbk)
ISBN: 978-1-315-51685-1 (ebk)

Typeset in Bembo
by Keystroke, Neville Lodge, Tettenhall, Wolverhampton

For Tom

CONTENTS

ILLUSTRATIONS

Figures

Tables

PREFACE

As an experiential, physical, material, embodied practice, one which brings mind and body together in the moment of 'making something', intellectual reflection is suspended. It is not a question of thinking 'I can't go there', but of working impulsively, imaginatively, creatively with the idea of: 'I can go here, there, everywhere'. And what happens if I go here? Do this? Say this? Creating is not about the limiting, but the limitless.

Elaine Aston, 2007, p. 14

It may seem strange to introduce a book about analytical thinking with a quote from feminist theatre scholar Elaine Aston about the need to suspend reflection in order to think imaginatively, but it allows me to jump right in to what I see as the core challenge facing those of us teaching and learning qualitative research. How do we make sense of the numerous analytical approaches used by qualitative researchers in a way that supports our own unique research agendas, while also encouraging us to stretch our thinking and to imagine research designs that go beyond the confines of our various disciplines? This requires, I believe, the need to think differently about the theory-practice relationship; replacing the idea of there being a right way to carry out a research study—which assumes that once the right way has been identified all one has to do is follow it—with a conceptualization of research as design-in-the-making; an approach that embraces re-vision and rethinking, and necessitates an introduction to the multiple theoretical and practical resources available.

What prompted the development of this book was a dissatisfaction with the resources available for teaching a general interdisciplinary course on qualitative analysis. While there are numerous and rich sources for types of analysis (for example, grounded theory, narrative analysis, critical ethnography), there are none that conceptualize the field of analysis from the analytical thinking strategies themselves; strategies that are embedded within these varied approaches but whose similarities and differences often become overshadowed by the methodological orientation shaping them. Furthermore, books taking a general, rather than a specific approach to qualitative research design present, for the most part, a limited view of qualitative analysis as coding and categorizing. Not satisfied with books that provide general introductions to analysis or focus on one methodology, I have used in my teaching a variety of sources, including exemplars of research using diverse methodological and theoretical approaches (for example, Condon, 2014, on the living experience of feeling overwhelmed and Cooper, 2007, on African-American mothers' decisions regarding the schooling of their children) and articles that deepen understanding of a specific analytic approach (for example, DeCuir & Dixson, 2004, on critical race theory and Flores-Kastanis, 2009, on participant action research). Additionally, Joseph Maxwell and Barbara Miller's (2008)[1] article on categorizing and connecting strategies for qualitative analysis, as well as Donald Polkinghorne's (1995) article on narrative configuration, provided good introductions to categorizing and narrative approaches to analysis, and aligned well with my belief that different forms of analysis represent different ways of conceptualizing what Jerome Bruner (1993) called "acts of meaning" (p. xii). Nevertheless, while both articles are excellent resources for understanding these two strategies for analysis, their presentations provide only a portion of the vast and messy analytic field, limiting rather than expanding students' analytical imaginations (Lather, 2006). Not wishing to tame the field but seeking ways to help students understand what they are doing when they do this thing called analysis, I have added three modes of thinking to the two identified by Maxwell, Miller, and Polkinghorne. Together, the five modes are: (1) Categorical Thinking; (2) Narrative Thinking; (3) Dialectical Thinking; (4) Poetical Thinking; and (5) Diagrammatical Thinking. Knowing that more exist and likely more are on the way, I believe, nonetheless, that these five ways of thinking present distinct forms of analysis that, while co-existing, are also critiques of one another.

Modes of Thinking for Qualitative Data Analysis, therefore, departs from the structure employed by other texts on qualitative research as it is neither a book on conducting qualitative research from beginning to end, nor does it provide procedures related to any one analytical approach, such as constant comparative analysis, or descriptions of the variety of methods linked to a specific methodology, such as narrative inquiry. Rather, the book aims to describe the actions and aims engendered by each mode of thinking in order to deepen researchers' conceptual understanding of these actions and aims. It is a conceptual analysis of analytical strategies and is built on the belief that imagination is essential to the analytic task. I agree with Maxine Greene (2001) that it is "imagination that enables us to challenge the fixed and the taken-for-granted, that allows us to open windows in the actual and disclose visions of what might be" (p. 110). Imagination is fueled when we consume the ever-expanding design configurations dreamed up by researchers near and far, and it is nourished by our own attempts to think differently about this practice called research. It is only in conversations with our data, with others, in person or virtually, and through exposure to how others think about research across the diversity of disciplinary conventions, that we can begin to break away from the narrowness of our own experiences and disciplinary roots. I hope this book provides students and instructors of qualitative research with an overview of the variety of analytical approaches in a way that supports new possibilities "where anything might happen" (Richardson & St. Pierre, 2005, p. 973).

Modes of Thinking for Qualitative Data Analysis, therefore, is a book about thinking. More specifically, it is a book about thinking about modes of qualitative data analysis as strategies that take on particular orientations depending on the theoretical perspective(s) guiding it. I purposefully do not tie them to any one theoretical perspective or methodology since theoretical perspectives (for example, symbolic interactionism, poststructural feminism, hermeneutic phenomenology), and methodologies (such as ethnography, action research, narrative analysis), take on different configurations depending on the specific problems they are meant to address. In other words, theories play a role in producing different strategies, but each strategy does not necessarily reflect back on, or represent the work of, any one theory. However, while the analytic strategies offered in this book are not directly tied to any one theoretical perspective, it is clear that each puts into action a particular epistemological orientation regarding the location of meaning and the aim of research. In other words, each responds to the question John Smith (1993) asked when differentiating one hermeneutic theory from another: "Where does meaning 'reside'"? (p. 185), and each describes a range of activities that constructs a particular enactment of meaning rather than another (Ezzy, 2002). Therefore, while each mode of thinking that is described draws from a variety of similarly-oriented approaches, what I depict in each chapter is an abstraction derived from an analysis of these approaches, and does not necessarily match any one theorist's version of the approach. As explained in the Introduction these are not models to follow but abstractions meant to serve thinking.

More importantly this is a book about understanding the contributions different modes of thinking are making to qualitative analysis. While scholars of qualitative research are drawing on a range of theoretical perspectives and methodologies, such as grounded theory, critical ethnography, phenomenology, multimodality, poststructuralism, and so on, most qualitative theorists who write about these design configurations do not do so in relation to the breadth of qualitative approaches available. They do, importantly enough, provide a much needed depth to particular theoretical and methodological approaches. Nevertheless, a challenge for instructors of qualitative research is deciding what text(s) to use in their teaching. This task is made more difficult in graduate level courses where the range of student interests and epistemological orientations often results in instructors needing to seek resources beyond those originally planned. This book is not intended to replace these other resources but, rather, to work alongside them as a way to convey the range of analytical strategies available. This book provides the conceptual ground from which to understand the variety of analytic options, as well as identifies the contributions different modes of thinking have made to the field of qualitative research. Furthermore, most studies use more than one analytical approach which makes the presentation of these strategies in one text fertile ground for qualitative design construction. In other words, understanding the actions inherent to thinking categorically or diagrammatically should enable researchers to consider how categorizing, for example, might contribute to other modes of thinking like dialectics. Putting these modes of thinking into dialogue with one another does not mean that their action or aim in each case will be the same. Quite the contrary, categorizing is going to serve a very different function in content analysis than it would when determining the parts of a plot for narrative analysis or identifying concepts in a poststructural document analysis. Overall, understanding the variety of modes of thinking for qualitative analysis is intended to support a deeper attention to analytic decision-making.

As an instructor I do not believe we learn by being given answers to problems. We learn when we are given opportunities to dwell in complexities. I also believe that we learn about our own theoretical stance when we are pushed to consider a variety of, often contradictory, positions. My approach to teaching and learning honors all of the modes of thinking presented in this book. Although I have my preferences, my intention is to help the reader see and value this range and not to make "categorizing look bad," as one of my students requested I mention in the Preface to this book. Her comment is especially helpful to remember because each mode of thinking is in many ways a critique of, and response to, the others, and so it would have been easy to tell a story of progress as I moved from categorizing to narrative and on to diagrammatical thinking. Instead, these are offered as equally important approaches to analysis with the hope that a deeper understanding of the kind of knowledge they produce will prompt researchers to think more critically about the limitations and potentials, and very different effects, each mode of thinking puts into motion.

Finally, I hope this book will demonstrate that attention to analytic strategies is a valuable approach to learning qualitative analysis. Although it is clear that the epistemological underpinnings of positivism, interpretivism, critical theory, and postmodernism are well-embedded in particular forms of meaning-making and the role of research in society, it is equally important to gain an understanding of these paradigms by analyzing the analytical practices employed by researchers. As Robert Donmoyer (2008) explains, paradigms "determine how members of research communities view both the phenomena their particular community studies and the research methods that should be employed to study those phenomena" (p. 591). I hope the descriptions provided in the next few chapters prove useful as students seek ways to locate themselves in the midst of the "paradigm proliferation" (Donmoyer, 1996; Lather, 2006) that characterizes qualitative research.

Modes of Thinking for Qualitative Data Analysis begins with an introductory chapter that situates thinking at the center of qualitative analysis, and analysis at the center of research design. Chapters 2, 3, 4, 5, and 6 each present one mode of thinking. These chapters begin with a general introduction to the mode of thinking followed by the characteristics that distinguish it as a unique analytic approach. Several research examples are then presented to illustrate how each mode of thinking *might* look in practice. They are not intended to be models for how that mode of thinking *should* be carried out. Again the intent is for readers to use examples to think critically about the possibility, as well as limitations, of different design decisions. Examples, whenever possible, are selected from high-quality, peer-reviewed journals and represent studies carried out in a variety of disciplines. Each chapter is concluded with a general commentary about the strengths and limitations of the mode of thinking in question. Chapter 7 outlines my pedagogical practice and concludes with an assessment of how well I feel *Modes of Thinking for Qualitative Data Analysis* covers the field.

Note

1 I am indebted to this article as it provided the premise from which this book was written.

References

Aston, E. (2007). Knowing differently: 'Practice as research' and the women's writing for performance project. *Nordic Theatre Studies*, *19*, 9–18.

Bruner, J. S. (1993). *Acts of meaning: Four lectures on mind and culture.* Cambridge, MA: Harvard University Press.

Condon, B. B. (2014). The living experience of feeling overwhelmed: A Parse research study. *Nursing Science Quarterly*, *27*(3), 216–25.

Cooper, C. W. (2007). School choice as 'motherwork': Valuing African-American women's educational advocacy and resistance. *International Journal of Qualitative Studies in Education*, *20*(5), 491–512. (DOI: 10.1080/09518390601176655).

DeCuir, J. T., & Dixson, A. D. (2004). "So when it comes out, they aren't that surprised that it is there": Using critical race theory as a tool of analysis of race and racism in education. *Educational Researcher*, *33*(5), 26–31.

Donmoyer, R. (1996). Educational research in an era of paradigm proliferation: What's a journal editor to do? *Educational Researcher*, *25*(2), 19–25.

Donmoyer, R. (2008). 'Paradigm.' In L. M. Given (Ed.), *The Sage encyclopedia of qualitative research methods* (Vol. 2, pp. 591–5). Thousand Oaks, CA: Sage.

Ezzy, D. (2002). *Qualitative analysis: Practice and innovation.* London, UK: Routledge.

Flores-Kastanis, E. (2009). Change at big school and little school: Institutionalization and contestation in participatory action research. *Educational Action Research, 17*(3), 391–405.

Greene, M. (2001). *Variations on a blue guitar: The Lincoln Center Institute lectures on aesthetic education.* New York: Teachers College Press.

Lather, P. (2006). Paradigm proliferation as a good thing to think with: Teaching research in education as a wild profusion. *International Journal of Qualitative Studies in Education, 19*(1), 35–57.

Maxwell, J. A. & Miller, B. (2008). 'Categorizing and connecting strategies in qualitative data analysis.' In P. Leavy & S. Hesse-Biber (Eds.), *Handbook of emergent methods* (pp. 461–77). New York, NY: The Guilford Press.

Richardson, L., & St. Pierre, E. A. (2005). 'Writing: A method of inquiry.' In N. K. Denzin & Y. S. Lincoln (Eds.), *The Sage handbook of qualitative research* (3rd edn., pp. 959–78). Thousand Oaks, CA: Sage.

Smith, J. K. (1993). 'Hermeneutics and qualitative inquiry.' In D. J. Flinders and G. E. Mills (Eds.), *Theory and concepts in qualitative research: Perspectives from the field* (pp. 183–200). New York, NY: Teachers College Press.

ACKNOWLEDGMENTS

Thanks go: To my brother, Steve, who generously allowed me to use a close-up of one of his works of art for the cover. The complete work (Diary, 2004) and others can be found at http://steve.litsios.org/portfolios/21/paper-works; to my parents, Susan and Socrates Litsios, for establishing a household where creativity in both the arts and sciences was nurtured and practiced; and to my brother, Ken, who showed us all how to take what life can throw at you with immeasurable dignity and optimistic strength. Thank you also to the anonymous reviewer who pushed me to take further what I had begun and engage more directly with the politics of research. Finally, I am indebted to two advisors in particular who fostered and modeled thinking in their students rather than conformity of thought: Louis Carini (Bennington College) and Sandra Mathison (SUNY Albany).

1

INTRODUCTION

Everything has the potential to be data, but nothing *becomes* data without the intervention of a researcher who takes note—and often makes note—of some things to the exclusion of others.

Harry Wolcott, 1994, pp. 3–4

In its becoming, the data is already multiplicitous—it is not dependent on being stabilised or known in an onto-epistemic project of qualitative research 'interpretation' and 'analysis.' As a machine, data 'works' when it enters and interrupts a flow, or is 'plugged in' to produce different ontologies.

Alecia Youngblood Jackson, 2013, p. 114

What these quotes make clear is that research does not come with built in directions; it needs to be designed (Maxwell, 2013). As such, it can be fluid, flexible and innovative, rigid, constrained and procedural, or, as in many cases, a combination of qualities. In all cases, however, it is strategic (even if the intent is to be non-strategic) in that it "attempts to think about actions in advance" (Freedman, 2013, p. x), but will modify those actions in response to new aims or unexpected events. Strategy, to me, best describes analysis because it suggests a dynamic decision-making process in-the-midst of the particularities of a data set, situation, aims and desires, rather than a predetermined procedure to follow. As strategist Lawrence Freedman (2013) explains: "By and large, strategy comes into play when there is actual or potential conflict, when interests collide and forms of resolution are required" (p. xi). What makes analysis challenging to novice researchers is that what is falsely assumed to be a procedure is fraught with conflicting interests. These conflicts have multiple sources. Some of them are internal to the researcher, such as prioritizing certain voices or themes over others, having a preference for certain modes of representation, and bringing preconceived ideas about how the world works and the role research plays in its working. Some are external, such as needing to communicate in a predetermined way to a committee or to other researchers in a field, or having to recruit participants in ways that alter the original aim or design of the study. And these negotiations do not end there. As Maxwell explains:

> You will need to continually assess how your design is actually working during the research and how it influences and is influenced by the context in which you're operating, and to make adjustments and changes so that your study can accomplish what you want.
>
> *Maxwell, 2013, p. 3*

So, from the start, it should be said that this is not a book about data analysis procedures, or a textbook with end-of-chapter questions. Although examples are used to illustrate the different modes of thinking that guide analysis, they should not be understood as *the way* to carry out any of the modes of thinking. They are not *models* of modes of thinking, but conceptualizations of the ways in which one or more modes of thinking have been put to use by social scientists. Furthermore, analysis is an interactive process. Strategies are not just applied *to* data; data prompt us, make us wonder, caution us, coerce us even into thinking certain ways. As Amanda Coffey and Paul Atkinson (1996) explain in *Making sense of qualitative data*: "There is no single right way to analyze qualitative data; equally, it is essential to find ways of using the data to think with" (p. 2). Additionally, I agree with Margot Ely, Ruth Vinz, Maryann Downing, and Margaret Anzul (1997) who write: "We think it is more important for researchers to understand certain principles underlying qualitative analysis and to adapt approaches as the needs of their own data suggest rather than to attempt to follow any one approach too rigorously" (p. 163). In this book, the descriptions offered of each mode of thinking, and the examples used to illustrate that mode in practice, are intended to assist in those negotiations and adaptations, and to help you better assess and understand what you are doing when you adopt certain analytical strategies over others.

New and innovative approaches to qualitative research continue to grow and enrich the possibilities for design facing qualitative researchers. No longer do popular definitions, based on a naturalistic perspective of qualitative research as an interpretive framework that prioritizes the meanings and perspectives of participants, prove sufficient. In fact, in the third edition of *The Sage dictionary of qualitative inquiry*, Thomas Schwandt (2007) argues that the term *qualitative* "does not clearly signal a particular meaning or denote a specific set of characteristics for qualitative research" (p. 248), which suggests that introducing the field with a definition might mislead rather than clarify. I like Norman Denzin and Yvonna Lincoln's (2011) statement that, even though it means "different things" in relation to different historical moments, "qualitative research consists of a set of interpretive, material practices that make the world visible" (p. 3), because it leaves the aim, concerns, strategies, values, and identification of what counts as data wide open, and supports the aim of this book which is to consider what each analytic approach might contribute to our understanding of the world. This is how I hope readers will approach the contents of this book, with a sense of wide-openness and curiosity. Furthermore, in assuming they have an introductory understanding of qualitative research design, this book was written with a desire to support and extend this understanding, rathers than to provide an introduction to qualitative design itself. However, it is likely that even with an introductory understanding of qualitative research readers will not be familiar with some of the approaches discussed in this book. That is fine. Just as Harry Wolcott (1992) suggested one should approach the collection of viewpoints offered in the first edition of the *Handbook on qualitative research in education* (LeCompte, Millroy, Preissle, Eds.) from the perspective of "a shopper" to see "what is available that may prove *useful to you*" (p. 5), this book encourages you to do the same. Think with these descriptions. Use them as points of departures for further perusing, reading, and reflecting. However, while the book encourages you to adapt and mix strategies, it is equally important to understand that as *modes of thinking* these configurations are not interchangeable, and cannot be changed like a pair of shoes. Rather, each puts into action particular ways of seeing and organizing the world, and, as such, alters what is taken to be the world itself.

Why Focus on Analysis?

All social scientific research involves a taking stock of what is being worked with and a process for making a statement about the topic of inquiry. In other words, all research involves some sort of data identification, organization, selection, creation, recognition, and some sort of transformation of what is identified, organized, selected, created, recognized into a statement about the topic of inquiry or "findings." The interaction between taking stock and making a statement can take many shapes, but it is always a "doing" with the intent of acting on a set of data in some way. When teaching analysis, I encourage my students to think critically about whether or not they are working with the kind of data, or the analytic approach, that will get them where they want to be. As Wolcott (1992) states: "To conduct any inquiry one must have both an idea of what one is attempting to accomplish and an idea of how to proceed" (p. 41). However, there are several challenges facing novice researchers that make producing a critical assessment of that task difficult. Briefly, these are:

1. Needing to do analysis to understand analysis,
2. Understanding the relationship between analysis and interpretation,

3. Understanding that writing is inseparable from analysis, and
4. Gaining enough exposure to diverse conceptualizations of analysis to imagine new possible configurations for research.

Chapter 7 discusses the first three challenges in relation to teaching and learning. Here I focus on the one directly addressed by this book: gaining enough exposure to diverse conceptualizations of analysis to imagine new possible configurations for research.

In order to embrace, and make use of, the range of configurations available to them, novice researchers need exposure to the diversity of approaches being put to use by interdisciplinary qualitative researchers, as well as a sense of the history of the field and its ongoing fight for legitimacy (Denzin & Lincoln, 2011). In other words, qualitative researchers must understand that research is "a technology of justification, meaning a way of defending what we assert we know and the process by which we know it" (Kincheloe, McLaren, & Steinberg, 2011, p. 169). Different forms of analysis make different claims to knowledge and result in different "truths." Without exposure to diverse conceptions of knowledge and truth, researchers run the risk of becoming deluded by their own worldview; believing it to be the one, and only, way to truth. To deepen our understanding of our own beliefs requires an awareness of those of others.

Inherent to my teaching, and one of the pedagogical principles of the Qualitative Research Program at the University of Georgia, is a belief in the value and power of interdisciplinarity. Interdisciplinarity best represents the multifaceted field of qualitative research which "crosscuts disciplines, fields, and subject matter" (Denzin & Lincoln, 2011, p. 3). Programs such as the one at the University of Georgia support cross-disciplinary conversation by serving an interdisciplinary body of students, and drawing on a cross-disciplinary range of theoretical and empirical literature. However, this does not mean that the methodological choices taught, and made in practice, are equally valid. So, while it is stated in the Preface that I do not want to make any of the modes of thinking look bad, neither do I endorse a relativistic position. Instead, I believe that relativism obscures the very real, beneficial and harmful, effects that particular research approaches have had on what individuals and groups believe to be true, meaningful, valid, and so on. Research, like teaching, is a political act, in that, as researchers or instructors, we make conscious decisions about what to include, exclude, emphasize, and strive for. Political scientist Andrew Douglas asserts:

> To think politically is to bring a set of evaluative or normative perspectives to bear on our reality. It is to conjure up, explicitly or implicitly, a set of imaginative projections about what our human situation can and should become.
>
> *Douglas, 2013, p. 43*

The five modes of thinking described in this book not only advance a critical awareness of the conceptual diversity inherent to the field of qualitative research, they also intentionally serve to disrupt the "qualitative positivism" (Prasad & Prasad, 2002, p. 6) narrowly endorsed by mainstream funding sources (St. Pierre, 2006). A focus on the analytical strategies involved in each mode of thinking makes visible the epistemological orientation and ontological assumptions they put into practice, and the ways in which they each shape the world in distinct, and often incompatible, ways.

Thinking, not Thought

A focus on thinking is not new. Philosophers, ancient and contemporary, have considered thinking to be a fundamental way of being in the world (Dahlin, 2009). Thinking is an intrinsic part of who we are, how we approach the world, and how the world itself gets produced. It is not something mechanical or external to ourselves that we pick up when needed. However, it is something we often do without awareness. It is in this indissoluble relationship of thinking and being that I try to make visible what it is that qualitative researchers do when they do this thing called "analysis." Focusing on thinking, therefore, is meant to bring to awareness the way different thinking modes enable different orientations; modes we inhabit and take on for a variety of reasons in our encounters as beings in the world. In qualitative research, thinking orients us to the task of being researchers, although it also risks being reduced to some sort of method, a process that can be followed. This book argues that this kind of reduction hurts our understanding of what it is that researchers do. So even while describing the modes of thinking as distinct, it is not for the purpose of fixing them as methods, but to enable their circulation, adaptation, and even, their transformation.

While I acknowledge that it is difficult, and often impossible or unnecessary, to make thinking visible, I believe there has not been enough emphasis on thinking within the literature on qualitative research (although recent publications suggest this is changing, see Jackson & Mazzei, 2012, and Saldaña, 2015). And although thinking cannot be taught, as it is itself "an activity expressing itself in many forms" (Dahlin, 2009, p. 548), it can be encouraged. I agree with Bo Dahlin (2009) who writes: "Contemplative practice is a way to learn to think, that is, to learn *to live consciously* in the *activity* of thinking" (p. 551). This conscious engagement requires a stance towards learning that simultaneously embraces reflective rumination and an active, critical engagement with different, and often difficult, presentations of meaning. Elizabeth St. Pierre (2011) explains: "If we don't read the theoretical and philosophical literature, we have nothing much to think with during analysis except normalized discourses that seldom explain the way things are" (p. 614). Providing an introduction to this selection of modes of thinking, however partial, is one way to encourage that engagement.

A Brief Introduction to the Modes of Thinking

The next five chapters describe in detail five modes of thinking for qualitative data analysis. These are: (*1*) Categorical thinking; (*2*) Narrative thinking; (*3*) Dialectical thinking; (*4*) Poetical thinking; and (*5*) Diagrammatical thinking. In this section, the modes of thinking and the kinds of questions each mode of thinking might encourage are briefly introduced using a data excerpt from my dissertation. As mentioned earlier, each mode of thinking provides analysis with a strategy aimed at doing something with data and, in turn, being able to say something significant about that data. A point to make clear is that while there is not one definition of qualitative research, I am working from the assumption that its aim is not to emulate methods of the natural sciences. Therefore, the modes of thinking presented here are best described as postpositivistic. As Prasad (2005) states: "In other words, they tend to approach questions of social reality and knowledge production from a more problematized vantage point, emphasizing the constructed nature of social reality, the constitutive role of language, and the value of research as critique" (p. 9).

For my dissertation, I conducted multiple interviews with 11 white parents from different social class backgrounds in order to examine the discourse of parental involvement through a close analysis of the narrative accounts of parents engaged in that practice. I was particularly interested in the way social class mediated parents' understandings, values, and actions regarding their involvement. The story selected here to introduce the modes of thinking is from Ellen's second interview with me. Ellen was a married working class mother, who graduated from high school and had taken some college-level classes. At the time of the study, her three sons were in grades one, four, and six in a public elementary school in a small town in the Northeast United States. During the interview I asked her about her activities and experiences with her children's school. When asked what she least appreciated about the school she told a story in which she felt communication between her family and the teacher was lacking. Without prompting she explained that what she valued most was open communication with school personnel, and she told this story to illustrate what she meant:

> My youngest son really acted kooky one day when there was a substitute and Mr. LeBlank (assistant principal) called me in. . . . This was the situation that happened. Anytime my son was told he couldn't do something he expects that the entire class can't do it; that what was good for one is good for the other, cause it goes the same way in our house. If they're all fooling around and they're not supposed to be then they're all in trouble. . . . Well there was this toy that my son had brought to school and he was asked to put it away, and he put it away. And then there were two other boys playing with toys, and so when the substitute

asked my son to put it away, my son said, 'well when you're asking me to put it away, what about them two over there, they're not allowed to have them out either.' 'You're being disrespectful,' the substitute said. My son said, 'you're being disrespectful to me because you told me to put it away and those two kids are over there playing with it and you're not telling them to put it away.' He said, 'you go back to your desk and put your head down.' When my son went back to his desk to put his head down there was a book, the teacher's book, so he went to put it back on the teacher's desk, and he was sent to the principal's office because he was out of his chair. And you know the substitute teacher is a man who wears his pants hiked up a little high, well my son was imitating him down the hall on his way to the principal's office, so when he got to the principal's office, [Mr. LeBlank said] 'I need to call your mom,' and he didn't really know the whole story. . . . So I went down. I said, 'yup, I'll be right there.' So I said 'I'm going to take my lunch break early. I just need to go over to Riverbed school.' And when I got there, we sat down, and I said to my son, 'you need to tell me exactly what happened, and don't lie to me. Just tell me the truth, I'm not going to be angry, we'll just talk.' Well he went on word for word everything that happened, and Mr. LeBlank called the substitute teacher down, and my son retold the story, and he said, 'well yes that is what happened.' So Mr. LeBlank was great. He said 'well you need to make sure that if one child is playing with a toy and is asked to put it back then the other ones need to put theirs away too because (son) does have a point.' So the whole situation was resolved. But you know I listened to what my son had to say and I feel yes he was disrespectful in the sense of making fun of that teacher, and I said 'we do teach you that you need to respect people and you should ask for respect from other people, but the way that you said it wasn't so cool with the substitute teacher.' So we talked about this thing, and it was a done deal.

Freeman, 2001a, pp. 142–3

What can one story tell us about parental involvement? While I believe it can tell us a great deal, the answer to this question is also determined by how our analytic questions and strategies give shape and direction to our findings. Since each mode of thinking prioritizes certain questions over others what counts as findings in each case will be articulated differently.

Categorical thinking serves a classificatory function for analysis. This is the kind of thinking that seeks to determine what something is, or is about, and creates order to the resulting categories. However, categories do not create themselves, and are often made up of other identifiable categories, so boundaries need to be established. Reading Ellen's story, I might ask: What is this an instance of? What other stories from Ellen, or other parents, does it belong with? For example, Ellen's story could be labeled "open communication" to align with how Ellen introduced it, or it could be labeled "school discipline practices" or "parental intervention" if I was grouping school disciplinary practices together or times when parents intervened somehow. Categories sort units of data into groups, so depending on what the other units of data suggest, I might be interested in the parts of the story that show family values, parents' ability to leave work at short notice, parents' accounts of their relationship with the school's administration, parents' interaction with their children, rule enforcement at home and at school, and so on. Categorizing helps to separate out units of data that can stand alone often as a way to contrast or relate them to other units of data. These labels can be fairly stable, or they can be fluid and temporary, depending on the overall design and purpose of the research.

Narrative thinking focuses on the construction or identification of theories of action or plots. Narratives connect and provide coherence to seemingly disparate events. This can take many forms, from analyzing the structure of narratives, such as the way Ellen tells this particular story, to analyzing her stories in search of "threads;" particular plotlines that are woven through a person's various accounts (Clandinin, 2013, p. 132). I might ask: What elements and actions are being brought together to form this story? Or, what kind of plotlines appear over and over in Ellen's stories, and what do they tell us about the kind of person she is presenting herself to be? In this way we might look more closely at the way she constructs her actions, those of her son, the teacher, and the assistant principal, and consider what is being accomplished in this telling, what kind of action moves the plot forward, what is its effect or meaning. Since narrative thinking helps researchers understand the actions and meaning-making processes of individuals, I might look across all the parents' stories in search of a better understanding of what matters to parents overall, what they believe about education and their roles as parents, or what they consider important to tell me, the researcher, about involvement.

Dialectical thinking seeks to uncover inherent tensions or contradictions that are believed to exist in humans as well as in societies, and put these in dialogue with each other for transformational purposes. While Ellen's story seems at first to be one of cooperation rather than conflict, another way of looking at this story is to wonder what kind of continuous effort on the part of Ellen, or the assistant principal, was needed to develop this type of collaboration or relationship. Furthermore, Ellen's presentation and her emphasis on family values and listening to her child, suggests that she believes these actions and beliefs may not necessarily be usual in other families or in how discipline is generally practiced in school. I might therefore focus on visible and hidden conflicting beliefs, and ask: What diverse values and beliefs are being negotiated in this account? What role does dialogue play in moving what was a punishable event into one with a solution or a desirable outcome for those involved? Dialectical thinking emphasizes transformation through a continuous process of dialogue or negotiation, so I might look at how Ellen positions herself in relation to others in the story, and how this position might be the result of negotiating less-than-desirable conditions for herself or her sons, and the belief that if these actions were not taken, things would return to a less-than-desirable state. Looking beyond Ellen, a dialectical researcher might wonder what these efforts look like for all the parent participants, and how parental intervention, in whatever form this takes, puts into motion different relationships for different people. Overall, a dialectical researcher would be interested in how practices such as parental involvement benefit and oppress those involved.

Poetical thinking focuses on those hard to reach felt experiences that transcend specific contexts and create forms of expression that expand and challenge the imagination. When we read a story like this one told by Ellen, we enter the flow of human understandings, experiences, and feelings; an aesthetic space that is our own, while also revealing threads and fragments of human meaning that transcend time and place. Researchers using poetical thinking strategies do not ask what this story means; rather, they ask, how does this story participate in the unfolding flow of meaning? What aspects of its telling contribute to a deepening of understanding of what it means to exist and perform as humans, and which aspects endure beyond this telling, to be told elsewhere, and in other forms? Poetical thinking asks us to blur the boundaries between art and research, to reject predetermined conceptions of what it means to "know," and to create research performances that expand and challenge the imagination. It asks us to allow for dramatic performances, for example, to consider ways in which this episode is "a path to consider what it is we humans are up to" (Richardson, 1998, p. 461), or to develop ways to work metaphorically with the content of the story. For example from Ellen's story I could expand analytically the idea of a "done deal" as being both the manifestation of the outcome of a business negotiation, and the distribution of a good like truth or justice. Or I could consider the way the story forms around a concept like the sharing of responsibility as a larger human theme. Poetical thinking approaches work with excesses of meaning that are only limited by the imagination and artistry of the researcher.

Diagrammatical thinking seeks to disrupt conventional ways of thinking about human and nonhuman interactive spaces or networks. It asks that we look beyond the familiar narrative construction of a story and transverse core aspects of its telling in a way that creates new assemblages of moving and rigid formations, junctures, and concepts. Diagrammatical thinking involves looking at change through intra-acting materializing bodies (Barad, 2007), rather than through preconceived concepts or forms of classification. Concepts such as "affect" which "refers to changes in bodily capacity" (Hickey-Moody, 2013, p. 80), or "desire" which is understood "as a coming together of forces/drives/intensities that produce something" (Jackson & Mazzei, 2012, p. 92) give some idea of the direction these analytic questions might take. I might ask: What are

Ellen, her story, my research desires, the discourse of parenting, involvement, educational achievement, social class, the notions of sharing responsibility, and so on, bringing into existence, becoming together? What is being produced at these junctures, and how does this production help me rethink the landscape of involvement? What makes diagrammatical thinking hard to describe is that it seeks ways out of the familiar systems of meaning, disrupts hierarchies between human and nonhuman agencies, and rethinks language and concepts as agential forces.

Modes of Thinking for Qualitative Data Analysis

The five modes of thinking offer five distinct strategies for qualitative data analysis. Table 1.1 outlines their purpose and focal actions. However, as discussed in the next section, their development is the result of co-existence and conversation, and is, therefore, best understood in dynamic relation, as they gain their identities from their critique of each other, as much as from what they each emphasize.

The Modes of Thinking in Dynamic Relation

History has shown that humans do not just live out their lives as passive recipients of some sort of fatal existence. From the beginning, being human has involved wondering about what this being is about. Our participation in the world has not only been an active one, but has played a large role in shaping, for good or ill, the very existence and world we wonder about. As a result there are many ways to research the world, each putting into practice different beliefs about the aims of research, beliefs about reality, and the strategies meant to connect the two. Analysis allows us to enter history, that is, to enter the changing flow of meaning, and participate in its construction. Separating this flow into five modes of thinking that have distinguished themselves from each other through a variety of strategic moves is one way of making sense of this participation. However, these modes of thinking are best considered in relation to one another. Figure 1.1 depicts the modes of thinking in relation.

In dynamic relation, one can begin to see the kinds of issues that have haunted social science researchers. What is the world made up of, and how should one inquire into it? Is data something to name and compare, select and connect into a harmonious whole, or is it more complex and chaotic? How should researchers engage in the activity of research? To what extent should these activities seek ways to minimize the effects of research itself? Or, on the contrary, since research produces effects, what effects are most, or least, desired? How should researchers intervene in history's shaping? Schwandt (1993) states: "What sets contemporary debates in social science apart are not methods debates but debates about the very substance of social science—large-scale

TABLE 1.1 Modes of Thinking for Qualitative Data Analysis

	Categorical Thinking	Narrative Thinking	Dialectical Thinking	Poetical Thinking	Diagrammatical Thinking
Overall Purpose	To create criteria from which to identify and organize data units.	To understand the activity of human meaning-making as unique theories of action.	To put into action a theory of change and rectify oppressive structures and practices.	To release hard-to-imagine ways of seeing and being into the flow of experiential life.	To engineer new articulations of the effects of turbulent encounters between diverse human and nonhuman particles.
Analytic Strategies	Identifying the criteria by which items are grouped into categories. Sorting objects according to some defining attribute or system. Comparing groups of objects to other groups of objects.	Highlighting the unique voice and meaning-making process of individuals and groups. Connecting disparate events into coherent plots. Examining human meaning-making as theories of action.	Identifying and critiquing co-constitutive oppressive relations. Surfacing and working the relevant points of discord in a continuous movement of negotiation in search of new relations. Constructing counter-stories meant to critique and overthrow oppressive practices.	Penetrating, listening, and circulating hard-to-articulate aesthetic meanings and understandings. Fusing artistry and research into provocative and poignant felt experiences. Creating expressions of encounters that expand and challenge the imagination.	Dissolving boundaries between preconceptualized systems of meaning. Reconceiving interactions (human and nonhuman) as transversal forces without foundations or predetermined aims. Materializing new agential relations in ways that generate new forms of thought.
Focus of Analysis	To determine what something is in relation to the conceptual scheme that gives it meaning.	To examine the way disparate events get connected in a particular context and from one or more points of view for one or more audiences.	To uncover inherent tensions that are believed to exist in humans and societies and put these in dialogue with one another for transformational purposes.	To perform difficult-to-grasp sensuous experiences in ways that reach beyond meaning and keep understanding in flow.	To unhinge established forms of thinking and map out forces acting through and emerging from entangled human and nonhuman assemblages.

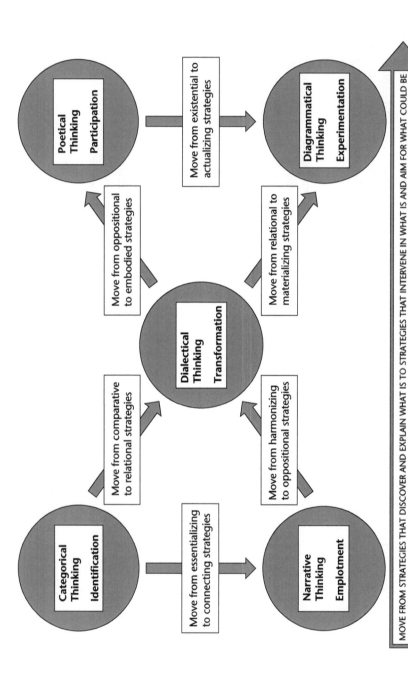

FIGURE 1.1 The Modes of Thinking in Dynamic Relation

disagreements about the nature, meaning, and purpose of human activity, including the activity of human inquiry" (pp. 10–11).

As Figure 1.1 demonstrates, there are varied perspectives on this issue. My exploration of the many ways research has been carried out revealed that this conceptualization has undergone many moves—more than can be addressed in any one book. It also made apparent the pivotal role dialectical thinking played in these theoretical conversations. As a theory of change, dialectics helped transform the aim of research from a focus on what is, or has been, to one where research is assumed to be an intervention; a focus on what could be. But, more importantly perhaps, dialectics revealed the potential of the generative space opened up by the dialectical friction itself, a generative space that has spawned a wide variety of dialectical approaches, and provided the ground for theorists seeking to transcend the perceived limitations of dialectics itself. As I illustrate in the chapters on poetical and diagrammatical thinking, these less familiar conceptualizations for research are dissolving familiar concepts, such as science and art, qualitative and quantitative, actual and virtual, and rewriting the field in new and creative ways. I believe that thinking in critical and creative ways helps challenge "the legitimation of existing forms of knowledge . . . [and create] an interruption through which difference makes its appearance in the world" (Duarte, 2009, p. 250). Ultimately, therefore, I hope a deeper understanding of the diversity that already exists in the field of qualitative research will not only support and inspire new forms of thinking for social science research, but further an appreciation for, and willingness to learn from, diversity itself.

Before turning to the modes of thinking in the following chapters, a few final points must be made:

- All modes of thinking described in this book already exist in the world and are used, to a greater or lesser extent, in everyday living and interacting. These modes are useful to us and serve us in many ways (for example, when we try to identify what something is: Is it a dog or a bear, an insult or a joke? When we are moved by a story of survival. When a complex work of art takes us beyond our own experience, and so on).
- Different cultures, disciplines, and groups of scholars have valued some modes over others. Some of these groups exist in comfortable dialogue with one another, while others must continuously strive to overcome rigid hierarchies of acceptance.
- In practice, the modes of thinking described in this book are often used in combinations. My intent in describing them separately is to illustrate their uniqueness, and demonstrate the theoretical assumptions that have given them shape. When used in combination or to do the work of a particular theoretical perspective, these assumptions often shift and change. My hope is that the descriptions provided in this book will encourage readers to recognize when, and how, these modes of thinking are being used.

- Finally, it is important to understand that the terminology used here does not necessarily match the definitions assumed by other scholars. The descriptions provided of the modes of thinking, although supported by what researchers do, are not always characterized in the same way. A researcher might approach narrative inquiry, for example, categorically, dialectically, poetically, or a researcher might use diagrams in their representations but may not be thinking diagrammatically in the way that is characterized here. Other terms could have been used in my presentation, but this would not have eliminated or reduced this issue.

References

Barad, K. (2007). *Meeting the universe halfway: Quantum physics and the entanglement of matter and meaning.* Durham, NC: Duke University Press.

Clandinin, D. J. (2013). *Engaging in narrative inquiry.* Walnut Creek, CA: Left Coast Press.

Coffey, A., & Atkinson, P. (1996). *Making sense of qualitative data: Complimentary research strategies.* Thousand Oaks, CA: Sage.

Dahlin, B. (2009). On the path towards thinking: Learning from Martin Heidegger and Rudolf Steiner. *Studies in Philosophy & Education, 28*(6), 537–54.

Denzin, N. K., & Lincoln, Y. S. (2011). 'Introduction: The discipline and practice of qualitative research.' In N. K. Denzin & Y. S. Lincoln (Eds.), *The Sage handbook of qualitative research* (4th edn., pp. 1–19). Thousand Oaks, CA: Sage.

Douglas, A. J. (2013). *In the spirit of critique: Thinking politically in the dialectical tradition.* Albany, NY: State University of New York Press.

Duarte, E. M. (2009). In the time of thinking differently. *Philosophy of Education Yearbook,* 250–2.

Ely, M., Vinz, R., Downing, M., & Anzul, M. (1997). *On writing qualitative research: Living by words.* Bristol, PA: The Falmer Press.

Freedman, L. (2013). *Strategy: A history.* New York, NY: Oxford University Press.

Freeman, M. (2001a). *Rearticulating the birthright of participation: Three tales of parental involvement.* Unpublished doctoral dissertation, State University of New York, Albany.

Hickey-Moody, A. (2013). 'Affect as method: Feelings, aesthetics and affective pedagogy.' In R. Coleman and J. Ringrose (Eds.), *Deleuze and research methodologies* (pp. 79–95). Edinburgh, UK: Edinburgh University Press.

Jackson, A. Y. (2013). 'Data-as-machine: A Deleuzian becoming.' In R. Coleman & J. Ringrose (Eds.), *Deleuze and research methodologies* (pp. 111–24). Edinburgh, UK: Edinburgh University Press.

Jackson, A. Y., & Mazzei, L. A. (2012). *Thinking with theory in qualitative research: Viewing data across multiple perspectives.* London: Routledge.

Kincheloe, J. L., McLaren, P., & Steinberg, S. R. (2011). 'Critical pedagogy and qualitative research: Moving to the bricolage.' In N. K. Denzin & Y. S. Lincoln (Eds.), *The Sage handbook of qualitative research* (4th edn., pp. 163–77). Thousand Oaks, CA: Sage.

Maxwell, J. A. (2013). *Qualitative research design: An interactive approach* (3rd edn.). Thousand Oaks, CA: Sage.

Prasad, A., & Prasad, P. (2002). The coming of age of interpretive organizational research. *Organizational Research Methods*, 5(1), 4–11.

Prasad, P. (2005). *Crafting qualitative research: Working in the postpositivist traditions*. Armonk, NY: M. E. Sharpe, Inc.

Richardson, M. (1998). Poetics in the field and on the page. *Qualitative Inquiry*, 4(4), 451–62.

Saldaña, J. (2015). *Thinking qualitatively: Methods of mind*. Thousand Oaks, CA: Sage.

Schwandt, T. A. (1993). 'Theory for the moral sciences: Crisis of identity and purpose.' In G. Mills & D. J. Flinders (Eds.), *Theory and concepts in qualitative research* (pp. 5–23). New York, NY: Teachers College Press.

Schwandt, T. A. (2007). *The Sage dictionary of qualitative inquiry* (3rd edn.). Thousand Oaks, CA: Sage.

St. Pierre, E. A. (2006). Scientifically based research in education: Epistemology and ethics. *Adult Education Quarterly*, 56(4), 239–66.

St. Pierre, E. A. (2011). 'Post qualitative research: The critique and the coming after.' In N. K. Denzin & Y. S. Lincoln (Eds.), *The Sage handbook of qualitative research* (4th edn., pp. 611–25). Thousand Oaks, CA: Sage.

Wolcott, H. F. (1992). 'Posturing in qualitative inquiry.' In M. D. LeCompte, W. L. Millroy, & J. Preissle (Eds.), *The handbook of qualitative research in education* (pp. 3–52). San Diego, CA: Academic Press, Inc.

Wolcott, H. F. (1994). *Transforming qualitative data: Description, analysis, and interpretation*. Thousand Oaks, CA: Sage.

2

CATEGORICAL THINKING

The human mind must think with the aid of categories. . . . Once formed, categories are the basis for normal prejudgment. We cannot possibly avoid this process. Orderly living depends upon it.

Gordon Allport, 1954, p. 20

The only reason why we think of categorical thinking as more logically compelling is that we feel more at home in it, as something of our own making. It is our instrument for coming to grips with what we think of as essential aspects of being.

Oliva Blanchette, 2003, p. 118

Introduction to Categorical Thinking

Categorizing is something we do every day when we identify or classify something as belonging to a particular group. It is an essential way of making sense of the world and an important part of social living. Any kind of language acquisition from birth onwards immerses us in learning categorical as well as variable linguistic forms (Nardy, Chevrot, & Barbu, 2013). As children learn to speak, they simultaneously learn the names of things around them, and during this process take note of the characteristics inherent to the thing named. This ability is astonishing and very young children are able to transfer the mental image of a dog seen on a walk to one seen within the pages of a book. They also quickly understand that everything has a word attached to it and they will ask for this if they cannot recall it or do not yet know it. Furthermore, children, just like adults, are capable of using language in abstract and non-literal ways (Gardner, 1974). Just consider everyday occurrences such as when my 32-month-old grandson called himself a "pillow" when his 10-month-old sister laid her head on his chest. It is clear that the word pillow was not understood literally as being simply the soft squishy thing for one's head but also as part of an action that defined it as a pillow. When thinking categorically, then, a pillow can belong to the category of "bedding" and to the category of "supports for one's head" and to other categories such as a "tightly stuffed material object." When we name something, we are, at the same time, framing it conceptually. This dynamic relationship between things, language, preexisting categories, and our ability to come up with new ways of conceptualizing and organizing the world, is at the core of categorical thinking.

In their study of thinking, psychologists Jerome Bruner, Jacqueline Goodnow, and George Austin (1956) concluded that a concept could be defined as "the network of inferences that are or may be set into play by an act of categorization" (p. 244). In other words, "a concept refers to a mentally possessed idea or notion, whereas a category refers to a set of entities that are grouped together" (Goldstone & Kersten, 2003, p. 600). Expanding upon the example of the pillow, when I glance around my living room I do not need to think twice about it being furnished with a table covered with books, and a couch. However, I could conceptualize these objects as a brown wooden surface, multiple colorful laminated surfaces, and a woven cotton, beige surface. Alternatively they might be conceptualized as the thing I put my feet on, the things I read, and the thing I sit on. Each of these ways of seeing provides an account of these three objects but draws upon different systems of classification. An essential component of categorical thinking, then, is that there is no agreed theory for determining the relationship between categories and concepts.

Since there is no standard way in which people make use of the multiple, mostly unconscious, and often competing, perceptual, cognitive, linguistic, and cultural factors available, categorizing can seem like "an act of invention" (Bruner et al., 1956, p. 2). This issue has fueled research in many areas related to philosophy, linguistics, and psychology, forming fields of study such as cognitive science, defined as "a cross-disciplinary enterprise devoted to exploring and understanding the nature of the mind" (Frankish & Ramsey, 2012, p. 1). Consider, for example, a core question in the study of perception: How is it that although humans can perceive the detailed hues and textures of a summer garden or the fine wrinkles of skin on a laughing face, they are content to register "garden" and "joy" to define them? Bruner et al. (1956) explain:

> The resolution of this seeming paradox—the existence of discrimination capacities which, if fully used, would make us slaves to the particular—is achieved by man's capacity to categorize. To categorize is to render discriminably different things equivalent, to group the objects and events and people around us into classes, and to respond to them in terms of their class membership rather than their uniqueness.
>
> *Bruner et al., 1956, p. 1*

For cognitive psychologists, categorizing is the human capacity for quickly discriminating from the available information the required level of detail for the task at hand. Bruner et al. (1956) explain that "in the case of most categorizing, we attempt to find those defining signs that are as *sure* as possible as *early* as possible to give identity to an event" (p. 13). Categorizing, therefore, is considered an adaptive mechanism that involves both an anticipation of the consequences of making an error, and an assessment about whether more information is needed. Going back to the example of the laughing face, a quick scan of the situation was probably all that was needed for the face to be interpreted as joyful rather than one which appeared threatening. Building on the interrelationship between language and culture and the categories used by a society, cognitive scientists have examined issues of learning, cognitive and linguistic development, stereotyping, communication, and so on, all of which have had a direct or indirect influence upon the theories and methods used by social science researchers.

Although the role categorizing plays may seem self-evident, seeing and explaining the world categorically was originally considered an innovation. Philosopher Isaiah Berlin (1978) explains:

> Kant was the first to draw the crucial distinction between facts—the data of experience as it were, the things, persons, events, qualities, relations, that we observed or inferred or thought about—and the categories in terms of which we sensed and imagined and reflected about them. These were, for him, independent of the different cosmic attitudes—the religious or metaphysical frameworks that belonged to various ages and civilisations.
>
> *Berlin, 1978, p. 7*

As Berlin goes on to explain, while Kant believed these categorical systems to be universal to all human beings, others concluded that there was too much variety between political and moral systems for there to be a permanent and stable system. Berlin believed that while there were "natural" or universal human categories, there were also cultural and moral categories, which he called "category-spectacles" (Crowder, 2004). Category-spectacles, according to Berlin, connect ill-defined realms of assumptions with meaning-making which is always "situated concretely in time and place" (Crowder, 2004, p. 192). In other words, how the world is conceptualized, that is, the category-systems that give it meaning, can create radically different perceptions, experiences, practices, and structures of existence, and, therefore, shape the meaning these experiences have for those who inhabit them.

Therefore, more interesting perhaps than how we learn to identify that something is a member of a category is the point that the labels we use for things give us insight into the different category systems, and "function as filters

. . . [providing] an excellent way of understanding the mental world of an individual, group, scientific community, or culture" (Goldstone & Kersten, 2003, p. 601). Whether concepts are thought to be grounded in perception, cognition or language, or in all of these things, it is important that the assumptions researchers make about what it is they are researching are clearly understood and stated. Since qualitative studies often draw on human accounts of the phenomenon studied, qualitative researchers must develop an understanding of the relationship between the account provided and the phenomenon studied. Two aspects of this relationship are particularly important. The first is that the process of categorizing involves viewing something *as* an identifiable something (Bruner et al., 1956; Goldstone & Kersten, 2003). In other words, humans do not just see or experience undefined and fleeting movements of shadow and light, but experience things as something perceivable and identifiable. Second, this is an interdependent relationship: the conceptual categories humans use to make sense of the world are constructed out of experience and, in turn, are used to make sense of experience. It is this mutually constitutive relationship, one that positions humans as interpretive beings, that makes categorizing a rich form of thinking for social science research.

Characteristics of Categorical Thinking

Categorical thinking serves a classificatory function for analysis (Polkinghorne, 1995). The analytic task is to locate or create "the category of which an item is a member" (Polkinghorne, 1995, p. 10). Categorical thinking attends to criteria and processes through which items are grouped into categories. Therefore, the primary purpose of categorizing is to identify the criteria for determining what something is, is made of, or is a part of. Identification or, more precisely, labeling things to define or order them, is its primary aim. The most common procedure for developing categories is to compare items and note their similarities. "Similarity-based relationships involve resemblances or common features . . . which can be independent of time and place" (Maxwell & Miller, 2008, p. 462). This process, which Polkinghorne (1995) calls seeking a category's "'specific difference,' . . . attends to the features or attributes that essentially define particular items as instances of a category" (p. 10).

Thinking categorically, therefore, includes consideration for the form of equivalency being used in the groupings, and their level of detail. For example, in a study of teachers' attitudes toward standardized testing, further differentiation based on age, gender, ethnicity, years of experience, educational program, teaching philosophy, geographical location, and so on, may or may not be relevant. Rationales for, or against, consideration of any demographic or other descriptors, while often considered part of any good study, are extensions of categorical thinking. Other forms of conceptualization might not determine these questions to be necessary or important. Therefore, part of the decisions involved in categorical thinking is to determine the level of detail needed for something to be a category, and whether or not a particular category will be somehow contrasted or related to other categories in the analysis.

A second characteristic of categorical thinking, then, is that most categories, by virtue of being, or made into, instances *of* something, are therefore at the same time *not* instances of something else. This quality of the category may seem self-evident but it is by determining its relationship to other items or units of meaning that the overall conceptual structure underlying the categories is made visible. For example, philosopher Rom Harré (1966) explains that Aristotle derived his system of categories "from the kind of questions that he thought it was possible to ask about anything" (p. 15). These questions included questions about substance, quality and quantity, relations and networks, and so on (Moravcsik, 1967). Harré argues that a key characteristic, therefore, of categorization is that it is "flexible, since it seems evident that we might find ourselves asking a new and different sort of question about any subject matter, and this would provide us immediately with a new taxon of concepts" (p. 15).

This highlights a third characteristic of categorical thinking—that it is intended to connect the particular to the general, conceptual, or formal (Polkinghorne, 1995). Bruner (1985) described this as a paradigmatic way of thinking. Paradigmatic thought fulfills the ideal of a formal, mathematical system of description and explanation. It is based upon categorization or conceptualization and the operations by which categories are established, instantiated, idealized, and related one to the other in order to form a system (p. 98). In other words, when researchers sort items or instances based on their similarities, they are creating distinctions between things based upon some characteristics over others. Categorizing, therefore, binds data units to mean this or that based upon the characteristics that are selected to define something as a *this* or a *that*. It is in this way that categorizing creates an abstraction of the thing itself. Its aim is "to generate general knowledge from a set of particular instances" (Polkinghorne, 1995, p. 14). More specifically:

> The realm of the particularity of each experienced item differs from the formal realm of concepts. The concept, apple, is not the same as an actual, material piece of fruit. The power of paradigmatic thought is to bring order to experience by seeing individual things as belonging to a category. By understanding that this particular item is an apple, I anticipate and act on the knowledge I have of apples in general.
>
> *Polkinghorne, 1995, p. 10*

So categorizing not only organizes things into groups but it also gives those things an identity as being a "this-kind-of-thing" rather than a "that-kind-of-thing." It provides a way to identify an item, trait, or action as belonging

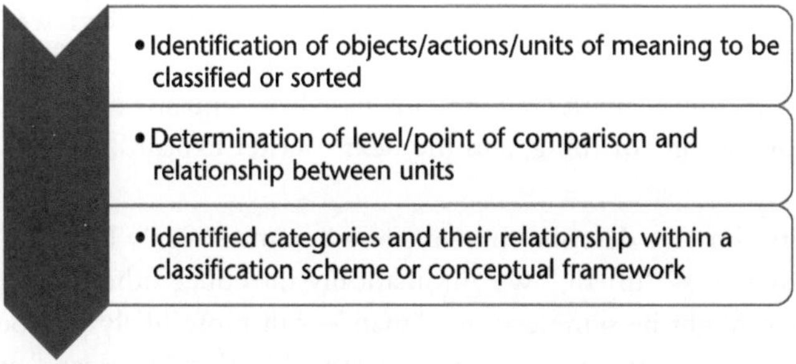

- Identification of objects/actions/units of meaning to be classified or sorted

- Determination of level/point of comparison and relationship between units

- Identified categories and their relationship within a classification scheme or conceptual framework

FIGURE 2.1   Connecting Categories to Concepts

to a certain group and a way of determining the relationship groups have to one another. Figure 2.1 depicts this process.

Categorizing supports theories of knowledge that assume that conceptual ordering of the world is not only attainable but useful for descriptive, explanatory, and, in some cases, predictive purposes. Identifying some things as fruit, others as disciplines, landscapes, affects, languages, and so on, allows humans to manage and navigate the world's never-ending flow of features, imagined or real. By producing "cognitive networks of concepts" (Polkinghorne, 1995, p. 10), humans make sense of the diversity and similarity of human responses simultaneously, recognizing instances as examples of broader human phenomena. This is a dynamic process as predetermined categories are used by researchers to explain certain behaviors, perceptions, and events and, in turn, these behaviors or events can serve to alter the parameters and meaning of a particular category.

This last point is one of the primary strengths of categorical thinking as well as one of its issues. While categories are not stable units (just think of how Pluto, a member of the category 'planet' since 1930 was re-categorized in 2006 when the definition of what constituted a planet was changed), they often become treated as such. Since a category is a decontextualized and simplified representation of a complex phenomenon, it is not always clear what other factors may have played an important role, making their use across contexts and cultures challenging and often problematic, a point expanded upon in the last section of this chapter.

Categorical Thinking in Practice

Categorizing is a useful strategy for research and is used in numerous ways. One area in which it is widely used is in studies where different kinds of characteristics or the constitutive parts of an experience are interesting in and of themselves (as opposed to narrative thinking where the relationship between parts constructs a coherent whole). Sociologist Howard Becker's description of the process for making sense of a series of photographs illustrates the analytical process involved in categorical thinking. He states that when we compare something to another we form tentative hypotheses about what the image, thing, and so on, is about. We do this based on similarities and differences between one image, or thing, and the next. Becker explains:

> Every time we describe someone as a "woman" or "white," or describe a situation as "urban," we automatically introduce other possible labels, which might be symmetrical—"man"—but more likely will be a list of coordinate alternatives: "black," "Asian," "Native American," and so on. If one situation is "urban," that points to other degrees of population density: "suburban" and "rural," maybe "exurban," perhaps others. The term we use alerts us to the existence of a dimension along which there are other positions than the one we've pointed to.
>
> *Becker, 2007, p. 48*

Researchers working categorically must therefore not only decide on what points of comparison are possible, but also what to name these. So although qualitative researchers often approach their data inductively, that is, by closely attending to the content of the data to guide the development of categories, this often involves the use of predefined and preexistent categorical schemes. Negotiating the relationship between pre-established concepts and dimensions, and a new set of data, therefore, is part of categorical thinking. Furthermore, in practice, categorical thinking is often used with other forms of thinking such as narrative or dialectical thinking. Therefore, to illustrate categorical thinking in practice, examples of studies were sought where categorical thinking took precedence over other forms of analysis. These examples also demonstrate different levels of negotiation between inductive and deductive procedures.

As part of her interest in labor market stratification processes, Lauren Rivera (2012) conducted a case study on the hiring decisions of elite banks, management, and law firms. Her data collection strategies consisted of interviews with 120 individuals involved in the hiring process from three different firms as well as conducting nine months of field work in one firm. During that field work, she was able to observe all recruitment events except for the job interviews themselves. Rivera provided a brief subjectivity statement to address how who she was might have affected the interviewees' responses: "I am an Ivy League educated female from a mixed ethno-religious background, which may have primed respondents to emphasize high-status cultural practices (which they did) and favor diversity (which they did not)" (p. 1005). Using an open, inductive analytic approach, she coded for all instances where evaluative mention was made about a candidate. It was during this process that the concept of "cultural fit" began to take shape. She explained that originally she had intended to focus her study on gender in hiring but, after noticing the relevance of fit in the hiring practices which she was observing, began to attend to this trend in her analysis also. Having determined that employers based their assessment of applicants upon some sense of likeness or compatibility, she had then to understand what kinds of similarities were most important. By comparing data units describing types of similarities with units describing their meaning and use, she was able to identify three categories of evaluative processes used to determine similarity: (*1*) "organizational processes" based on "cultural fit"; (*2*) "cognitive processes" based on the "valuation of candidates' qualifications"; and (*3*) "affective processes" which provoked interest and excitement in the interviewer (p. 1006).

Categorical thinking supported Rivera's aims of understanding the criteria used in the hiring practices of these elite firms by helping her to sort through the evidence and organize it in order to support her findings. Constructing categories allowed her, first, to identify cultural fit as a significant concept, second, to organize the data units into representative categories, and third, to rank these categories based upon their frequency of use. It was in this way that she was able to conclude that cultural matching was a significant factor in the decision-making process. In her presentation of findings she provided an account of all three processes as well as considering alternative explanations for her findings. She concluded her analysis by restating the importance of cultural matching as well as by showing its relationship to the other processes.

Another example of categorical thinking is provided by Anna Rowe, Julie Fitness, and Leigh Wood's (2015) examination of the role of emotions in learning and teaching in higher education. They took a social-functional approach to the study of emotions which assumes that emotions affect how people act and cope in particular settings. Looking specifically at positive emotions, the research questions guiding their study were: "What effect, if any, according to participants, do positive emotions have on learning (i.e. outcomes)? What types of learning situations are associated with positive emotions (i.e. antecedents)?" (p. 3). Participants for the study included an interdisciplinary group of faculty (15 in total) and students (21 in total) attending a university in Australia.

In order to answer their research questions, Rowe et al. needed to think about how they would account for the variety of emotion descriptors used by participants. In order to do this they, first, coded the participant interview transcripts inductively, using the participants' own terms of emotion (for example, satisfaction, pride, passion) and, second, grouped these under preexisting categories developed in Shaver, Schwartz, Kirson, and O'Connor's (1987) prototype analysis (namely, joy/happiness, interest/excitement, love, self-consciousness, relief). To make sure I understood what this meant, I returned to Shaver et al.'s (1987) article in which they described this approach. They explained that prototype theory developed by psychologist Eleanor

Rosch in the 1970s was meant to address the "fuzzy" nature of the category sets used in everyday life. Shaver et al., state:

> Each of these fuzzy categories is defined, not by a conclusive set of necessary and sufficient features. . ., but rather by a *prototype*—an abstract image or set of features representing the. . . most typical example of the category (e.g., the "prototypical" chair). Categorization decisions are made by comparing instances with this prototype.
>
> *Shaver et al., 1987, p. 1062*

The interviews conducted by Rowe et al. (2015) with university students and instructors were semi-structured and meant to elicit responses on specific emotion themes such as relationship and motivation. After coding was completed, the data were then grouped under themes (for example, "cognitive and social functioning" and "motivation" to consider the effects of emotions, and "passionate inquiry" and "individual variables" to consider their sources) in order to answer the research questions and relate the findings back to the social-functional theoretical framework. Categorical thinking was used strategically to guide both the deductive and inductive procedures used in this study. This allowed the researchers to manage variability in meanings that are believed to accompany emotion terms in a way that supported the aims of the study, which were to examine "discrete emotions in learning contexts, rather than broader positive affect more generally" (p. 15).

Coding as a means to identify units of data and sort them into categories is a common strategy for carrying out categorical thinking in practice. Using an inductive approach takes advantage of the dynamic interpretive movement between identifying something as the member of a category, and altering the category structures used to organize the data into findings. Sociologist Kathy Charmaz explains:

> Coding means that we attach labels to segments of data that depict what each segment is about. Through coding, we raise analytic questions about our data from the very beginning of data collection. Coding distills data, sorts them, and gives us an analytic handle for making comparisons with other segments of data.
>
> *Charmaz, 2014, p. 4*

Although this description is taken from her book on the subject of grounded theory, which if done from the beginning using theoretical sampling puts into action a form of narrative thinking, many studies using the method of grounded theory, the constant comparative approach, aim to develop themes which are often, but not always, guided by categorical thinking.

Deciding on Categorical Thinking for Analysis

It is impossible to conduct any kind of research without using some form of categorizing. Just the act of selecting a topic, recruiting participants, and deciding on relevant concepts involves categorizing.

In general, categorizing helps researchers to:

- Identify something as a member of a group
- Reduce the complexity of a data set
- Sort objects according to some defining attribute
- Compare objects to other objects

However, when categorical thinking is employed as the primary analytical strategy, it is important to be aware of its strengths and limitations in order to identify the analytical conditions for which it is best suited. As noted throughout this chapter, categorical thinking is a useful strategy when identification of significant patterns, and comparisons between entities or groups, are the aim of research, and it has provided support for research seeking to deepen the understanding of concepts deemed significant to a particular field. What has not yet been discussed are some of the criticisms leveled at categorical thinking, criticisms that have resulted in the development and adoption of other modes of thinking, such as those described in the next few chapters.

The overall purpose of categorical thinking is to identify or create criteria from which to categorize data units. While the examples used so far in this chapter may not appear controversial, many, if not most, categories employed by social scientists have a normative effect; that is, there is an assumed "normal" or "usual" from which to compare variations. George Herbert Mead (1934) reminds us that language itself "does not simply symbolize a situation or object which is already there in advance; it makes possible the existence or the appearance of that situation or object, for it is a part of the mechanism whereby that situation or object is created" (p. 78). This is an important point regardless of the mode of thinking adopted, but especially provocative when assessing the benefits and harms of an approach aimed at defining data units in particular ways. Three of the most cited concerns directed at categorical thinking strategies are: the inherent bias of language, the essentializing nature of categories, and the resulting decontextualization of the concepts created. These three issues are inherent to the process of categorizing, which means that while they cannot be eliminated, researchers will want to make careful decisions about the categories they use in relation to the claims they make. A lack of attention or awareness can result in researchers inadvertently developing, or keeping in circulation, concepts that are considered harmful, oppressive, or problematic in some way.

The bias of language. Since the categories and concepts we use as researchers make visible our beliefs and what matters to us, they also reflect deep-seated biases we have about ourselves and others. Sport sociologist Robert Rinehart remarks:

> As we know from Foucault, how we choose to name other people and groups—how we categorize them—often tells us more about us, about our stance on how things are, than it does about any truth of who they are.
>
> *Rinehart, 1998, p. 201*

For example, how social scientists have used the concept of race, which is believed not to have any biological bearing (Graves, 2001), says much about our society's stance on racial diversity, our attitudes towards ourselves and others, and the way such naming has infiltrated our disciplines and discourses. Social psychologist James Jones explains this concern:

> *Race*—this four-letter word has wreaked more havoc on people in the world than all the four-letter words banned by censors of the U.S. airwaves. Race divides human beings into categories that loom in our psyches. Racial differences create cavernous divides in our psychological understandings of who we are and who we should be.
>
> *Jones, 1997, p. 339*

Becker (1998) explains that our commonsensical notions about the world, that is, what we feel we already know about it, constrain our abilities to change how we see, and think about, the object of our study. He laments: "How can we know and take account in our analyses of the most basic categories constraining our thought, when they are so 'normal' to us that we are unaware of them?" (p. 83). Although strategies for resisting the tendency to prioritize well-established categories are beyond the scope of this chapter, qualitative designs are well-positioned to critique and re-define these categories since their aim is often to develop new understandings rather than to confirm established ones. Nevertheless, qualitative researchers must continuously question the assumptions about what they take to be normal and seek ways to upset conventionalized ways of thinking (Becker, 1998). One way of doing this is to continuously attend to the potential consequences of the concepts or categories used, whether considered beneficial or damaging, and note the effects their use might have on particular individuals, groups, norms, and disciplines.

The essentialist nature of categories. Another criticism leveled at categorical thinking is that it is reductionist. Since part of its process is to construct identifiable and comparable categories out of complex events, the result is a reduced and simplified version of their components. A primary concern here is that these essentialized descriptions become "a surrogate for being" (Bhaskar, 1993, p. 355), resulting in the categories and concepts themselves standing in for complex events and interactions. When this occurs, concepts used in everyday practices become taken-for-granted as something true and natural far removed from the grounds and reasons for their conceptualization. In addition, the process of narrowing entities to identifiable categories often results in the creation of static and unified identities for things that may be better understood as being made of conflicting and complex, but necessary parts (Bhaskar, 1993), a concern that provides support for dialectical strategies.

Faulty generalization. Third, but related to the previous two criticisms, is that the desire to create generalizable categories or concepts means that often categories used to describe certain people or behaviors get transferred from context to context, resulting in the loss of the specific contextual features needed for making appropriate claims. Cultural anthropologist Mariko Fujita (1991) explains that this can result in "the use of a single perspective in comparing different cultures" (p. 21). Concepts such as "the self" or definitions of other popular categories may not be relevant or conceptualized in the same way by different people or cultures which, she says, "poses a vexing problem for those of us conducting cross-cultural research. Before we can compare two cultures, we need some kind of criterion for comparison; and yet the criterion is precisely what is called into question" (p. 20). A fundamental error occurs when categories or concepts are assumed to be inherently valid and considered applicable to any set of data without reflecting on their history and effect. For example, identity categories can be especially problematic. Consider this example by philosopher Emmanuel Eze who as an Igbo Nigerian describes his experience of coming to the United States as a graduate student and needing to fill out identification forms to receive a social security number.

> The forms I was required to complete asked me to indicate which race I belonged to. I searched for 'Igbo' but in vain. Instinctively, I turned over the form, looking for instructions as to a larger category under which the Nigerian Igbos might have been subsumed, but nothing prepared me for what I found: Nigerians are black all right, but not Algerians, who were categorized as white; the Sudanese are black, but not the Egyptians; and while the Zanzibarians of Tanzania are black, Libyans are white; and so forth.
>
> *Eze, 2001, p. 218*

To understand the history of classification systems, such as this one, requires looking beyond our assumptions about ourselves and others and into the political, social, economic, and cultural conditions that constructed such a system. Eze asks: "How can we think about the limits of our own systems of racial classifications—those structures of mind so naturalized and automatic that we usually don't even think about them at all?" (p. 219). These are the kinds of questions researchers using categorical approaches must ask themselves.

The major critique, then, of categorical thinking is that it organizes complex entities into systems of categories that create a knowledge structure far removed from its source. Researchers using categorical thinking who wish to minimize these issues seek ways to situate their research in particular contexts, address the limitations of their studies in a reflexive manner, or combine categorical strategies with other, more dynamic strategies, such as narrative or dialectical ones.

References

Allport, G. W. (1954). *The nature of prejudice.* New York, NY: Addison Wesley.

Becker, H. S. (1998). *Tricks of the trade: How to think about your research while you're doing it.* Chicago, IL: The University of Chicago Press.

Becker, H. S. (2007). *Telling about society.* Chicago, IL: The University of Chicago Press.

Berlin, I. (1978). *Concepts and categories: Philosophical essays.* New York, NY: The Viking Press.

Bhaskar, R. (1993). *Dialectic: The pulse of freedom.* London, UK: Verso.

Blanchette, O. (2003). *Philosophy of being: A reconstructive essay in metaphysics.* Washington, DC: The Catholic University of America Press.

Bruner, J. S. (1985). 'Narrative and paradigmatic modes of thought.' In E. Eisner (Ed.), *Learning and teaching the ways of knowing* (pp. 97–115). Chicago, IL: The University of Chicago Press.

Bruner, J. S., Goodnow, J. J., & Austin, G. A. (1956). *A study of thinking.* New York, NY: John Wiley & Sons.

Charmaz, K. (2014). *Constructing grounded theory* (2nd edn.). Thousand Oaks, CA: Sage.

Crowder, G. (2004). *Isaiah Berlin: Liberty, pluralism and liberalism.* Cambridge, UK: Polity Press.

Eze, E. C. (2001). *Achieving our humanity: The idea of the postracial future.* New York, NY: Routledge.

Frankish, K., & Ramsey, W. M. (Eds.) (2012). *The Cambridge handbook of cognitive science.* Cambridge, UK: Cambridge University Press.

Fujita, M. (1991). The diversity of concepts of selves and its implications for conducting cross-cultural research. *Anthropology and Humanism, 16*(1), 20–2.

Gardner, H. (1974). Metaphors and modalities: How children project polar adjectives onto diverse domains. *Child Development, 45,* 84–91.

Goldstone, R. L., & Kersten, A. (2003). 'Concepts and categorization.' In A. F. Healy & R. W. Proctor (Eds.), *Comprehensive handbook of psychology. Volume 4: Experimental psychology* (pp. 599–621). Hoboken, NJ: Wiley.

Graves, J. L. (2001). *The Emperor's new clothes: Biological theories of race at the millennium.* New Brunswick, NJ: Rutgers University Press.

Harré, R. (1966). 'The formal analysis of concepts.' In H. J. Klausmeier & C. W. Harris (Eds.), *Analyses of concept learning* (pp. 3–17). New York, NY: Academic Press.

Jones, J. M. (1997). *Prejudice and racism* (2nd edn.). New York, NY: McGraw-Hill.

Maxwell, J. A., & Miller, B. (2008). 'Categorizing and connecting strategies in qualitative data analysis.' In P. Leavy & S. Hesse-Biber (Eds.), *Handbook of emergent methods* (pp. 461–77). New York, NY: The Guilford Press.

Mead, G. H. (1934). *Mind, self, and society: From the standpoint of a social behaviorist.* Chicago, IL: The University of Chicago Press.

Moravcsik, J. M. E. (1967). 'Aristotle's theory of categories.' In J. M. E. Moravcsik (Ed.), *Aristotle: A collection of critical essays* (pp. 125–45). New York, NY: Anchor Books.

Nardy, A., Chevrot, J.-P., & Barbu, S. (2013). The acquisition of sociolinguistic variation: Looking back and thinking ahead. *Linguistics*, 51(2), 255–84.

Polkinghorne, D. E. (1995). Narrative configuration in qualitative analysis. *International Journal of Qualitative Studies in Education*, 8(1), 5–23.

Rinehart, R. (1998). Fictional methods in ethnography: Believability, specks of glass and Chekhov. *Qualitative Inquiry*, 4(2), 200–24.

Rivera, L. A. (2012). Hiring as cultural matching: The case of elite professional service firms. *American Sociological Review*, 77(6), 999–1022.

Rowe, A. D., Fitness, J., & Wood, L. N. (2015) University student and lecturer perceptions of positive emotions in learning. *International Journal of Qualitative Studies in Education*, 28(1), 1–20.

Shaver, P., Schwartz, J., Kirson, D., & O'Connor, C. (1987). Emotion knowledge: Further exploration of a prototype approach. *Journal of Personality and Social Psychology*, 52(6), 1061–86.

3
NARRATIVE THINKING

Narrative demarcates, encloses, establishes limits, orders. And if it may be an impossibly speculative task to say what narrative itself is, it may be useful and valuable to think about the kinds of ordering it uses and creates, about the figures of design it makes. Here, I think, we can find our most useful object of attention in what has for centuries gone by the name of plot.

Peter Brooks, 1984, p. 4

A story . . . must be more than just an enumeration of events in serial order; it must organize them into an intelligible whole, of a sort such that we can always ask what is the "thought" of this story.

Paul Ricoeur, 1984, p. 65

Introduction to Narrative Thinking

As the opening quotes suggest, thinking narratively involves constructing plots, and is another strategy used by humans to make sense of, and create order in, their worlds. Narrative theorists generally agree that without plot there would be no identifiable narrative or story. "Plot is the principle of interconnectedness and intention which we cannot do without in moving through the discrete elements—incidents, episodes, actions—of a narrative" (Brooks, 1984, p. 5). Consider, for example, the meaning behind this set of statements: "the teacher called me," "you would think," "a picture of the states," "it was wrong." Although we may easily imagine these statements as a narrative, they only became a narrative when we connected them as such. So while there may be different definitions of what constitutes a narrative or story, for the purposes of this chapter, I am viewing narrative as an outcome of Peter Brooks's "principle of interconnectedness" in whatever form that may take. As Brian Richardson (2000) explains, regardless of the variety of narrative forms and purposes, "narrative is a representation of a causally related series of events" (p. 170), where "causally" refers to any kind of meaning-producing or explanatory connection made in the constructed tale. Returning to the aforementioned loose statements, these were extracted from a story told by Lisa, a mother of two who began her response to my opening question about her own school experience by telling me she had dropped out of school in tenth grade and now regretted it. Over the next few questions she built an explanation as to why she dropped out by tying together a need for more time to learn, and negative experiences she had experienced with in-class participation. When I asked her if a particular event stood out for her, she told me this story:

> Um, well I can remember one time the teacher called me up (laughs) and she had a picture of like the States (Me—hmhm) but they didn't say the names of them, and she wanted me to find a certain one. And I'm up there going 'yup ok I can't do this,' so I just pointed one out, and (laughs), it was wrong and the whole class just laughed at me. And you would think that the teacher would have said something, you know like 'that was rude,' but no, just 'go back to your seat and study,' and that was all. It's like I just wanted to go curl up into a corner and just hide. You know, it's like, I mean at least the teacher could have said something to the kids like 'well that's not right, you shouldn't laugh,' you know, 'we're all here to learn.' That's what I'd say, you go to school to learn not to be laughed at, and if you're laughed at you're not going to learn anything.
>
> *Freeman, 2001a, p. 181*

Lisa told me many stories during three interviews on the topic of parental involvement. These stories went back and forth across time and context. She used stories like this one to explain her actions and decisions as a parent in relation to her children's schooling or to make sense of her children's school experiences. Narrative inquirers believe that we tell others about ourselves through stories and that the process of telling stories is a way to make sense of our lived existence. However, as historiographer Hayden White (2001) explains: "We do not *live* stories . . . we give our lives meaning by retrospectively casting them in the form of stories" (p. 228). Furthermore, the capacity to tell and to understand stories is believed to be something all humans are, to a greater or lesser extent, capable of. "This is a form of intelligence that . . . does not require the apprehension of general principles and causes. Rather, it is an 'implicit understanding' that originates from experience and remains within the horizon of particular events and situations" (Carli, 2015, p. 106). It is this human capacity as narrators, and consumers, of stories that results in narrative thinking being so compelling an object of study, *and* in its development as a form of analysis for the social sciences.

Accepting narratives as a legitimate form of thinking, however, has required a continuous and interdisciplinary effort on the part of scholars in the human and social sciences. Literacy scholar David Olson (1990) explains that during the classical era, a clear distinction was created between "unreflective, uncritical" narrative forms of expression which were "taken as the antithesis of thought . . . [and] logical argument and prosaic discourse . . . [which] have continued to dominate our conceptions of thinking to this day" (p. 99). Fortunately, challenges to what has been called, among other names, the "rational-world paradigm" (Fisher, 1987, p. 47) or the "paradigmatic" or "logico-scientific paradigm" (Bruner, 1985, 1986) have significantly altered the ontological and epistemological landscape in the social sciences, and have had a deep influence on narrative having a central place in qualitative research. The belief that narratives play a significant role in the human world and constitute a valid means for making sense of human existence is, now, for the most part, well-established in the humanities and the social sciences (Clandinin, 2007; Polkinghorne, 1988; Riessman, 2007). What is focused on in this chapter, however, is not narrative inquiry per se, but emplotment: the mode of thinking that characterizes much, but not all, of the research incorporating some aspect of narrative into the design. "Plot as I conceive it is the design and intention of narrative, what shapes a story and gives it a certain direction or intent of meaning" (Brooks, 1984, p. xi).

Another way to think about this is that plot is "the 'element' that imitates *praxis*" (Carli, 2015, p. 105), where *praxis* is understood in the Aristotelian way as being the practical domain of action. To understand a plot, one needs to be able to understand the way action unfolds in a given account, and the complex ways various events and characters intersect with these actions, whether what constitutes *action* is a series of events or a reflective account. It is important to note here that while humans tell stories, and these stories are often the focus of inquiry, narrative thinking is also an analytic approach that aims to convey the result of inquiry through plot. How one theorizes the purposes and sources for what constitutes a plot varies. Therefore, regardless of who tells the story, researcher or participant, it is important not to assume that all theorists adopt the same foundation for narrative thinking. In other words, it is important not to conflate the intent of the narrator with what gets narrated.

Characteristics of Narrative Thinking

We are surrounded by stories and construct stories as we make sense of the events we live and witness. Our stories are often embedded in other stories, which are themselves embedded or linked to other stories. This unending flow of meaning-making affects, and is affected, by human existence, whether or not we pay attention to it. Indeed, "the emplotment of events into narrative form is so much a part of our ordinary experience that we are usually not aware of its operation, but only of the experience of reality that it produces" (Polkinghorne, 1988, p. 160). Thinking of this vast interconnected material through emplotment is what characterizes narrative thinking. Therefore, a stance is required on what is meant by emplotment when narrativizing strategies are used in research. In other words, whether talked about as "resonant threads" (Clandinin, 2013), "identity" (McAdams, 1988), or "existentials" (van Manen, 1990), it is essential for researchers to understand *what* they are plotting, and *how*. This section discusses some of the assumptions that explain the what, while the section on practice considers the how.

Scholars working in a variety of disciplines have conceptualized narrative emplotment in different ways. This is why a psychologist might be interested in what narrative plots convey about identity, a philosopher might worry about narrative and metaphysics, and a scholar of communication might wonder what a particular narrative is communicating, and how that "message" is being received. Overall, however, one reason narratives are considered significant to understanding human existence is because an understanding of narrative requires interpretation, and interpretation is believed to be how humans orient themselves to the world. As such, narratives are manifestations of these interpretive capacities and require interpretation to access their meaning(s). Explaining his interest in plotting, rather than in plots, Brooks (1984) remarks that plotting concerns "the activity of shaping, with the dynamic aspect of narrative—that which makes a plot 'move forward,' and makes us read forward, seeking in the unfolding of the narrative a line of intention and a portent of design that holds the promise of progress toward meaning" (p. xiii). Taking this out of the context of literature, a focus on plotting helps us to understand how narrative "operates as an instrument of mind in the construction of reality" (Bruner, 1991, p. 6), or how "a chronicle or listing of events [is transformed] into a schematic whole by highlighting and recognizing the contribution that certain events make to the development and outcome of the story" (Polkinghorne, 1988, pp. 18–19). Additionally, narrative thinking is based on the belief that narrative structures or plots reflect a basic human tendency, which is to connect events, characters, circumstances, decisions, and so on, in a way that provides meaning to that experience. Therefore, narrative thinking, or what Maxwell and Miller (2008) call contiguity-based analytical processes "involve juxtaposition in time and space, the influence of one thing on another, or relations among parts of a text; their identification involves seeing actual *connections* between things, rather than similarities and differences" (p. 462). Furthermore, this form of thinking is action-oriented and purposeful in that the "unified whole" (Polkinghorne, 1995, p. 11), which is the outcome of constructing a plot, is believed to be constituted around a human need to know how to act in the social world.

In other words, plots are dynamic in that "narrative texts themselves appear to represent and reflect on their plots" (Brooks, 1984, p. xii), and invite an audience (whether directly or indirectly) to participate in their unfolding. We do this actively, although often unconsciously, ascribing motives to actions, making connections between events, and continuously revising our understanding even while the narrator tells us otherwise. Therefore, there is no single way to think about emplotment. There are, however, some shared characteristics. Since narratives are a representation of the way a series of events have been connected, attention to connective operations used in narratives, for example, the way time is depicted, or a series of actions, or the motives behind the characters' actions, become important clues as to the narrative's intent or effect. Furthermore, narratives are told and written in a variety of contexts and for a variety of purposes, so these, too, must be accounted for when considering what sense can be made of a particular plot. For example, speaking about the narrative work of historians, White (2001) suggests that historians must take into account "the *types* of configurations of events that can be recognized as stories by the audience for which . . . [they are] writing" (p. 224). Similarly, literary critic Barbara Smith (1980) criticizes the decontextualized approach taken by narratologists who focus solely on the structure of a text and argues that all stories are "manifest, material, and particular retellings—and thus versions—of those narratives, constructed, as *all* versions are, by someone in particular, on some occasion, for some purpose, and in accord with some relevant set of principles" (p. 218).

When we construct a story we gather together a variety of linguistic, physical, historical, geographical, sensual, physiological, cultural, and relational materials. Even when asked to "state the facts" about an event, our interest in conveying a "believable" or "truthful" account means that we not only add rhetorical elements to our telling, but also convey the story from a particular point of view. When we read a novel or an historical account, it is easy for us to overlook the historical and cultural conditions that surrounded its creation. But another equally important context to consider is that our reading of the novel or historical account also plays a role in its shaping. Who we are and where we are located historically, culturally, and geographically shapes the story that is being told as well as the way the story is read and interpreted. It is for this reason that Smith (1980) prompts us to understand narratives "as part of a *social transaction*" (p. 232) so that we pay close attention to the circumstances surrounding the telling of a story, and not just view it purely as an inert text. And White (1992) agrees that "conflict between 'competing narratives' has less to do with the facts of the matter in question than with the different story-meanings with which the facts can be endowed by emplotment" (p. 38). The resulting conflicting accounts of supposedly factual affairs continue to pose interpretive challenges to historians and social scientists, prompting some to criticize narratives for their unreliability, while others argue that narrative thinking provides crucial insights into human interpretation (see Munslow, 2007, for one account of this debate).

Another characteristic of narrative thinking is that when we tell a story, or reflect on a story told, we always do so from a particular perspective, meaning that its uniqueness is always in relation to *something outside of itself*. This "something outside of itself" has been variously conceptualized (for example, tradition, culture, lifeworld, intersubjectivity), but is believed to be the webs of meaning we all participate in—albeit in different ways—that provide the basis for our capacity to understand each other.[1] Nick Crossley explains:

> Intersubjectivity is the key to understanding human life in both its personal and its societal forms. It is that in virtue of which our societies are possible and we are who we are. . . . [I]t is something that we cannot step out of. . . . We are inter-subjects.
>
> *Crossley, 1996, p. 173*

This interaction between the particular and the general provides qualitative researchers with a strong argument for the social scientific value of studying a small number of cases in detail. The focus on narrative detail provides researchers a unit of analysis that allows them to examine human meaning-making in context, while also providing the theoretical basis for considering that the narrative form taken encompasses, or puts into actions, values and meanings that are considered variations of a broader shared human existence.

Another explanation is that a focus on the unique case or story is an essential source of what Gary Thomas (2010) calls "exemplary knowledge" which, he argues, is an "example viewed and heard in the context of another's experience . . . but used in the context of one's own" (p. 578). Although not always theorized as such, the crafting of stories is a form of practical reasoning. "Practical reason is the general human capacity for resolving, through reflection, the question of what one is to do" (Wallace, 2009, n.p.). Furthermore, Polkinghorne explains:

> the recognition or construction of a plot employs the kind of reasoning that Charles Peirce called "abduction," the process of suggesting a hypothesis that can serve to explain some puzzling phenomenon. Abduction produces a conjecture that is tested by fitting it over the "facts." The conjecture may be adjusted to provide a fuller account of the givens.
>
> *Polkinghorne, 1988, p. 19*

Whether the stories are one's own or those of others, they provide "a basis for understanding new action episodes by means of analogy" (Polkinghorne, 1995, p. 11) and are considered a dynamic resource for individual and social

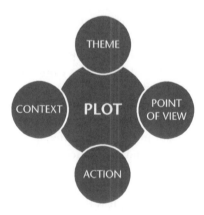

FIGURE 3.1 Dimensions of Plot

change. Since stories are themselves dynamic and are told differently depending on the reason for, or context of, the telling, they also provide potential for re-emplotment. In other words, narratives can help bring order out of chaos, provide explanations for unexpected events, and also spark reflection, critique, and rearticulation of events.

Finally, while there are recognizable narrative genres (for example, comedy, tragedy, satire, and so on), a plot is not something predetermined and imposed upon disparate events; it is something presented to us in the narrative unfolding itself. So another shared feature across theories is the way in which telling a story is understood as an act and, therefore, requires a theory of action (van Dijk, 1975). Teun van Dijk explains: "Whereas 'doings' are real, extensional objects, actions are *intensional objects*, to be identified by our *interpretations* and *descriptions* of doings" (p. 281). One could say, therefore, that a plot is the manifestation of a particular theory of action. It is the way a sequencing of events (action) unfolds in regards to particular or global circumstances or issues (theme) in a particular time, place, location (context) from one or more point of views and for one or more audiences (point of view). Figure 3.1 depicts these dimensions.

What differentiates narrative thinking from categorical thinking is the way in which plot mediates events and understandings across, time, place, and cultural context and puts into action a unique point of view about an event of significance. Philosopher Brian Fay explains:

[Narratives] show us how various actions and events led forward one to another toward a particular end. The significance of each action is understood in terms of its role in an unfolding drama. In these and countless other cases, particular acts are related to other particular acts not as instances of a certain general law, but in their particularity as each pushes forward a continuing line of transformation.

Fay, 1996, p. 170

Research on narrative, therefore, has contributed to the development of many interpretivist theories of action for the social sciences. It has done this by arguing:

- that humans have stories worth telling
- that any story, no matter how similar to others, is unique in one way or another
- that regardless of how unique or different a story is from others, it provides an important perspective on human existence in general
- that it is in this mediation between the particular and the general that much can be learned about the interpretive capacities of individuals as well as the historical, social, discursive, linguistic, and cultural materials that give shape to human interpretations
- that plotting, by virtue of never being static, is both evidence of, and potential for, human change.

In other words, whether a plot mediates across time and place, between events, or between speakers within a text or in relation to the narrator, one of its unique contributions is how this mediation provides social science researchers with a way in which to theorize an interdependent relation between the particularities of human existence and the general condition of being human.

Narrative Thinking in Practice

Making story-telling a central feature of research has a well-documented presence in the social sciences and has brought to light several assumptions associated with working in narrative modes. First, stories, whether written or oral, have, as far as we can tell, always existed as part of the social world. Second, a story told does not necessarily correspond to a story lived. Third, stories, however theorized, bring people together across time, place, and culture. Fourth, and related, stories transcend time while also being meaningful in time; their significance manifesting itself over and over in a variety of ways for multiple contexts. The possibilities inherent in narrative plotting are endless so, similarly to the section on categorical thinking, studies have been selected that demonstrate a variety of ways in which narrative thinking could be used in analysis, whether or not they draw explicitly on narrative theory as a framework.

Since narrative thinking is believed to provide coherence to the stories people tell about their lives and decisions, narratives are often elicited and analyzed as a way to understand a particular topic or phenomenon. Sheri Price, Linda Hall, Jan Angus, and Elizabeth Peter's (2013) narrative study of millennial generation students' nursing career choices provides an example of this kind of study. They believed that knowing more about why millennial students chose nursing would contribute to a better understanding of this generation of young people and assist with recruitment and retention in the profession. They argued that "understanding career choice using narrative theory requires attending to the process of emplotment, how individual events are linked together, with particular attention to context, language and temporality" (p. 307).

Participants included 12 female students who had been accepted onto a Canadian Bachelor of Science in Nursing program. Each participant was interviewed twice and attention was maintained on the narrative structure of their accounts. Using a combination of narrative and categorical thinking, their analysis involved mapping the plots of each story and identifying general themes. Several shared themes were identified and the theme of focus in this article, "Emplotting Career Choice Around the Virtues of Nursing," was presented through a rich description of the subthemes thought to constitute it: "Making a Difference," "Characterizing Self as Nurse," "Imagining Nursing as the Ideal Career," and "Constructing Choice as a Calling" (p. 308). In this way, "career choice was represented as a course of discovery and understanding more than a static moment in time or definitive event" (p. 308). Each subtheme was understood, and presented, as a significant part of the actions and choices made by the nursing students in relation to choosing nursing as a career. Throughout the narrating of each subtheme the authors tied their findings back to narrative theory as a way to support their analysis.

In this study, and in others like it, narrative theory provided the epistemological basis for theorizing narrative emplotting as a way of understanding and knowing (Ricoeur, 1984). As mentioned earlier, narrative thinking helps humans make sense of, or give order to, the "multiple and scattered events" (Ricoeur, 1984, p. x) of their lives. Researchers drawing on narrative theory argue for the centrality of narratives as a way to examine human-centered phenomena such as experience (Clandinin & Connelly, 2000) or different conceptions of identity (Bamberg, De Fina, & Schiffrin, 2007), and use narrative thinking as an analytic approach that provides legitimacy to the analytic decisions made, and to the presentation of the findings.

Narrative thinking as an analytic approach is fairly common in qualitative research studies but is not always labeled as such, or used within an explicit narrative framework. Polkinghorne describes this analytical approach:

> [This] kind of investigation is *explanatory*; its aim is to construct a narrative account explaining "why" a situation or event involving human actions has happened. The narrative account that is constructed ties together and orders events so as to make apparent the way they "caused" the happening under investigation.
>
> *Polkinghorne, 1988, p. 161*

Emir Estrada and Pierrette Hondagneu-Sotelo's (2011) study of Latino immigrant youth street vendors provides an example of narrative analysis. They wanted to understand why Latino youths would "consent to spend all summer and most of the school year pushing a cart with cut-up fruit through blazing city streets" (p. 111). It was hard work and there were many pressures—from peers, the law, and society—that would easily explain why they might not have consented to this work. Less evident was why they would. Using data collected from nine months of field observation and interviews with 20 Latino youths aged ten to 21 (mostly of Mexican heritage and female), Estrada and Hondagneu-Sotelo reconstructed an account of the youths' reasons for street vending, as well as their responses to the stigma the work carried.

Their findings wove together their observations and the young people's accounts, in the form of a "narrative explanation" (Polkinghorne, 1988) of the economic and moral reasons provided by the youths, and the difficulties and rewards of working as street vendors to contribute to their family income. Understanding why did not yet help the researchers understand how the youths "cope[d] with the responses of others who may tease them or disparage them" (p. 116). So adding to the unfolding narrative for why the Latino youths consented to this kind of work even though it went against the norm, Estrada and Hondagneu-Sotelo showed how the young people constructed "affirming narratives of intersectional dignities" (p. 117), which served to set themselves apart from the negative, mostly criminalized, images of Latino youth circulating in society, and differentiated themselves from non-working Latino youth who they perceived as "lazy" or "spoiled" or acted "as though they were white" (p. 118).

Like all research accounts, not all the young people interviewed recognized themselves in the above narrative. For some, street vending felt uneasy, was something to be kept secret, and did not reflect the kind of work they desired. Estrada and Hondagneu-Sotelo contextualized their findings and acknowledged the strengths and weaknesses of their design and analysis.

In examples like this, narrative thinking as a theory of action grounded in the data provides support for research aimed at answering "why" questions, such as, for example, grounded theory studies. Charmaz (2014) explains: "Theories offer accounts for what happens, how it ensues, and may aim to account for why it happened. Theorizing consists of the actions involved in constructing these accounts" (p. 228).

Because of its dynamic and action-oriented nature, narrative thinking has also contributed to the performative turn in the social sciences (Conquergood, 1989). Julie-Ann Scott's (2011) study on the personal stories of physically disabled professionals provides an example of a study looking at narratives as performances. As Scott stated, a performative approach provided "a vehicle to understand how professional narratives are created through performativity, emerging through daily *embodied interactions*, even as cultural discourses of professionalism seek to render bodies irrelevant" (pp. 238–9).

Scott recruited and interviewed "26 self-defined physically disabled professionals from 14 different states . . . for a study seeking to learn: '*What it means to be a physically disabled professional situated in cultural discourse*'" (p. 241). As a physically disabled professional herself, she was particularly interested in the way her participants' bodies were implicated in their professional work stories, whether or not they themselves were conscious of these interactions. Scott explained: "Performance analysis attends to how all narratives are the creation of bodies interacting in time and space, co-constituting performativities, in their reiteration, resistance, and/or dismantlement of the meanings that emerge from them" (p. 240). Her analysis of her participants' stories needed, therefore, to account for both what her participants told her, and how their stories provided evidence for different enactments of bodily performances within professional situations. Using Super Hero narratives (for example, Super, Warrior, Tragic, and Rogue) helped her provide the narrative logic of each performed identity, and although she illustrated these with her participants' accounts, participants do not embody any one particular Super Hero identity; these were enacted situationally. "Physically disabled professional heroes are not located within particular bodies but are cultural constitutions that surface in interaction, performances emerging from the perceived absurdity surrounding physically disabled professional identity" (Scott, 2011, p. 255).

Beginning with the assumption that bodies are performative, Scott analyzed the transcripts taking note of how the stories were being told with regard to tone, gestures, or laughter, what was being emphasized, what transitions were used, and so on. Additionally, she focused on "three levels of narrative positioning" (p. 242). These included relations to others in the story, relations to the audience or researcher, and relations to self. This process, Scott explained, helped her identify the different kinds of body performances as they manifested themselves in different situations and in relation to different positionalities. Using short narratives to illustrate the positions described, Scott made visible the way her participants' bodies played a central role in the telling of the stories.

In general, constructing plots provides a way to retain the unique circumstances of a person's experience, an organization's journey of change, or the historical conditions surrounding an event, and can be used with a variety of design options. So whether the researcher traces the unique plot of a speaker or constructs a plot out of disparate data sources, value is placed on the uniqueness of each situation and what can be learned about human nature from an analysis of these unique conditions. Because of the complexity of the interrelation between the research story and the stories told within a study, as well as the emphasis social science and qualitative research places on human action and interaction, narrative thinking is ubiquitous as a mode of thinking, and can be found across disciplines in a variety of forms.

Deciding on Narrative Thinking for Analysis

The turn to narrative is a turn to human agency, a subjective way of knowing which is thought to be more relevant to issues affecting human beings. Like other modes of thinking it has its strengths and limitations. One of its primary strengths for analysis is the familiarity of its form; the way narrative emplotment figures centrally in everyday human talk. Therefore, narrative thinking develops from and uses well-known narrative conventions. Ethnographer Bud Goodall describes these conventions well:

> The story's narrative and rhetorical supporting structure (for example, its form or genre, episodes, passages, conflicts, turning points, poetic moments, themes, and motifs) are constructed out of ordinary and extra-ordinary everyday life materials that, from a reader's perspective, allow meaningful patterns to emerge and from which a relationship develops.
>
> *Goodall, 2000, p. 83*

With its focus on human action, narrative thinking allows researchers to:

- Connect disparate events into coherent accounts
- Witness the unique variations of human experience-making by attending to the way individuals put into action their own interpretive "principles of interconnectedness"
- Highlight human practical domains of action or *praxis*
- Connect individual experiences to universal human themes

Although narrative thinking has gained popularity and legitimacy across disciplines, it is not without its own issues. And, for the most part, these all revolve around its subjective and interpretive nature, whether the narrative accounts are provided by research participants or constructed by researchers themselves. In general, researchers working with narrative strategies will want to consider the issues of correspondence, coherence, and culture.

Correspondence. Narrative theorist, Mark Freeman (2010) explains that drawing on narratives in social science research has always raised questions about the "relationship between life as lived, moment to moment, and life as told, in retrospect, from the vantage point of the present" (p. 3). In a general sense there is agreement among narrative researchers that all narratives are "an unstable mixture of fabulation and actual experience" (Ricoeur, 1992, p. 162). However, researchers disagree with how much each is needed for narrative research to be considered valid. For example, narrative theorists disagree about how (or whether) to address issues of memory, intended or unintended distortions on the part of participants, or how to account for multiple versions of the same story if some form of correspondence to the actual experience is required for their study. For some researchers, such as historians, these issues are of critical importance. When researchers are interested in individuals' perspectives on their own lives it might not matter at all whether the accounts happened in the way described, but when those accounts clash with versions told by others, then whose truth should take precedence? Whose account should be considered more valid, reliable, worth telling? And what criteria should be used to determine which history to tell ourselves and our children? Since our understanding of the past depends on what we have lived or what we have been told of it, the past and its telling can become entangled in the politics of science in complex ways (see Friedländer, 1992, for example, for a collection of essays on the complicated issue of representing the Holocaust). Therefore, depending on the context, the narrative decisions we make can have serious consequences. This is one reason that most narrative theorists call for transparency in regards to the interpretive decisions made in the process of constructing a research report (Etherington, 2004). Furthermore, many theorists believe that by ignoring the interpretive and literary procedures used in the research process the abilities of researchers and historians to engage issues of representation collectively has weakened (White, 2001).

Interestingly, even when correspondence is dismissed as irrelevant and narratives are not believed to mirror reality, there is still widespread reluctance towards the writing of fiction as research (Watson, 2011). Watson states that "[t]his reluctance is no doubt the result of a deeply felt need for research to be grounded in an empirical reality of something that *really happened*" (p. 396), even if that happening is understood as one person's version of the truth. Nevertheless, in practice there are researchers who are turning to fiction as a viable means of representing social science research findings (Clough, 2002; Watson, 2011; Whitebrook, 2001). While much of this work employs narrative thinking, the move for others from action and intention as a focus to one of immersion in felt experience, positions their work as primarily driven by poetical thinking, an approach described in Chapter 5.

Coherence and Culture. Coherence, and what counts as coherence, is another issue facing narrative researchers. In general, "narrative is capable of representing fragmentation, disunity, uncertainty and of offering solutions to what would otherwise be disabling disjunctions" (Whitebrook, 2001, p. 87). However, coherence is always "an interpretation of some aspect of the world that is historically and culturally grounded and shaped by human personality" (Fisher, 1987, p. 49). So while a story can draw on a wide variety of rhetorical strategies, what counts as a story is rooted in tradition, and these traditions do not necessarily align with one another. This means that what counts as a coherent account is always tangled up with the politics of culture (Benhabib, 2002).

Narrative scholars must, therefore, attend to this intersection, both in their decisions about what narratives to report and how to craft these, but also in the way in which they articulate a rationale for narrative research. The reason for this is that there are crucial distinctions, and disagreements, among narrative researchers regarding the role and agency of the narrator, the role and position of the researcher, and whether narratives can analytically stand alone or must be positioned within broader discursive, cultural, or political frameworks. In other words, while narrative researchers tend to agree that narratives are legitimate forms of experiential knowledge (Clandinin & Connelly, 2000; Collins, 2009), they differ regarding the role and emphasis of the dimensions of plot depicted in Figure 3.1. Although a description of the varieties of narrative theories is beyond the scope of this chapter, like categorical thinking, some of the possibilities and constraints offered by narrative thinking are inherent to the mode of thinking itself.

For example, a fundamental part of the process of emplotment is to transform complex events into coherent, organized accounts. Since what counts as coherence is not only determined by linguistic conventions, but is also at the mercy of cultural, social, and disciplinary norms, the stories that get circulated and accepted are more often those that reinforce, rather than resist, the status quo. This issue makes narrative research vulnerable to the same criticisms leveled at categorical thinking. Nevertheless, narrative thinking's emphasis on the principles of interconnectedness and its grounding in everyday practice, provide a strong argument for the validity of first person accounts as a reliable source of knowledge about an event lived and witnessed by the narrator (Collins, 2009). The strength of narrative thinking is in its ability to make visible the interpretive capacities of human agents in relation to their actions, interactions, beliefs, and practices. As such, narrative thinking is not only considered an important way to understand human action and experience, but has become a core component for critical, emancipatory research, a form of research most often guided by dialectical thinking, the topic of the next chapter. This is because, as some have argued, it is not narrative's connection to culture per se that is the issue, but when researchers seek to classify and represent these in ways that silence culture's inherent multiplicity (Benhabib, 2002). Benhabib explains: "The lived universe of cultures always appears in the plural. We need to be attentive to the positioning and repositioning of the other and the self, of 'us' and 'them,' in this complex dialogue" (p. 41). A challenge, then, for researchers making use of narrative thinking is how to contextualize situated or cultural stories in ways that maintain the inherent complexity of an individual's or a group's understandings. Taking a dialectical approach has been one solution to this issue.

Note

1 The importance of the influence of these webs of meaning continues in dialectical, poetical, and diagrammatical thinking but is taken up differently. Whereas in dialectical thinking, the tensions produced between the structures of meaning and the material productions of lived life as experiences or discourses become the focus of analysis, in poetical and diagrammatical thinking, the lifeworld, experience, etc. is not an entity that preexists the meaning encounter or event itself, but becomes manifest during the course of that event.

References

Bamberg, M., De Fina, A., & Schiffrin, D. (Eds.) (2007). *Selves and identities in narrative and discourse*. Amsterdam, The Netherlands: John Benjamins.

Benhabib, S. (2002). *The claims of culture: Equality and diversity in the global era*. Princeton, NJ: Princeton University Press.

Brooks, P. (1984). *Reading for the plot: Design and intention in narrative*. New York, NY: Alfred A. Knopf.

Bruner, J. S. (1985). 'Narrative and paradigmatic modes of thought.' In E. Eisner (Ed.), *Learning and teaching the ways of knowing* (pp. 97–115). Chicago, IL: The University of Chicago Press.

Bruner, J. S. (1986). *Actual minds, possible worlds*. Cambridge, MA: Harvard University Press.

Bruner, J. (1991). The narrative construction of reality. *Critical Inquiry, 18*, 1–21.

Carli, S. (2015). 'Aristotle on narrative intelligence.' In A. Speight (Ed.), *Narrative, philosophy and life* (pp. 103–18). Berlin: Springer.

Charmaz, K. (2014). *Constructing grounded theory* (2nd edn.). Thousand Oaks, CA: Sage.

Clandinin, D. J. (Ed.) (2007). *Handbook of narrative inquiry: Mapping a methodology*. Thousand Oaks, CA: Sage.

Clandinin, D. J. (2013). *Engaging in narrative inquiry*. Walnut Creek, CA: Left Coast Press.

Clandinin, D. J., & Connelly, M. (2000). *Narrative inquiry: Experience and story in qualitative research*. San Francisco, CA: Jossey-Bass.

Clough, P. (2002). *Narratives and fictions in educational research*. Buckingham, UK: Open University Press.

Collins, P. H. (2009). *Black feminist thought: Knowledge, consciousness, and the politics of empowerment*. New York, NY: Routledge.

Conquergood, D. (1989). Poetics, play, process, and power: The performative turn in anthropology. *Text and Performance Quarterly, 1*, 82–95.

Crossley, N. (1996). *Intersubjectivity: The fabric of social becoming*. London: Sage.

Estrada, E., & Hondagneu-Sotelo, P. (2011). Intersectional dignities: Latino immigrant street vendor youth in Los Angeles. *Journal of Contemporary Ethnography, 40*(1), 102–31.

Etherington, K. (2004). *Becoming a reflexive researcher: Using our selves in research*. London, UK: Jessica Kingsley Publishers.

Fay, B. (1996). *Contemporary philosophy of social science: A multicultural approach*. Malden, MA: Blackwell.

Fisher, W. R. (1987). *Human communication as narration: Toward a philosophy of reason, value, and action*. Columbia, SC: University of South Carolina Press.

Freeman, M. (2010). *Hindsight: The promise and peril of looking backward*. New York, NY: Oxford University Press.

Freeman, M. (2001a). *Rearticulating the birthright of participation: Three tales of parental involvement*. Unpublished doctoral dissertation, State University of New York, Albany.

Friedländer, S. (Ed.) (1992). *Probing the limits of representation: Nazism and the final solution*. Cambridge, MA: Harvard University Press.

Goodall, H. L. (2000). *Writing the new ethnography*. Lanham, MA: AltaMira Press.

Maxwell, J. A., & Miller, B. (2008). 'Categorizing and connecting strategies in qualitative data analysis.' In P. Leavy & S. Hesse-Biber (Eds.), *Handbook of emergent methods* (pp. 461–77). New York, NY: The Guilford Press.

McAdams, D. P. (1988). *Power, intimacy, and the life story: Personological inquiries into identity.* New York, NY: The Guilford Press.

Munslow, A. (2007). *Narrative and history.* London, UK: Palgrave Macmillan.

Olson, D. R. (1990). 'Thinking about narrative.' In B. K. Britton & A. D. Pellegrini (Eds.), *Narrative thought and narrative language* (pp. 99–111). Hillsdale, NJ: Lawrence Erlbaum Associates.

Polkinghorne, D. E. (1988). *Narrative knowing and the human sciences.* Albany, NY: State University of New York Press.

Polkinghorne, D. E. (1995). Narrative configuration in qualitative analysis. *International Journal of Qualitative Studies in Education, 8*(1), 5–23.

Price, S. L., Hall, L. M., Angus, J. E., & Peter, E. (2013). Choosing nursing as a career: A narrative analysis of millennial nurses' career choice of virtue. *Nursing Inquiry, 20*(4), 305–16.

Richardson, B. (2000). Recent concepts of narrative and the narratives of narrative theory. *Style, 34*(2), 168–75.

Ricoeur, P. (1984). *Time and narrative, Volume 1* (trans. by Kathleen McLaughlin and David Pellauer). Chicago, IL: University of Chicago Press.

Ricoeur, P. (1992). *Oneself as another* (trans. by Kathleen Blamey). Chicago, IL: The University of Chicago Press (originally published in French, 1990).

Riessman, C. K. (2007). *Narrative methods for the human sciences.* Thousand Oaks, CA: Sage.

Scott, J.-A. (2011). Attending to the disembodied character in research on professional narratives: How the performance analysis of physically disabled professionals' personal stories provides insight into the role of the body in narratives of professional identity. *Narrative Inquiry, 21*(2), 238–57.

Smith, B. H. (1980). Narrative versions, narrative theories. *Critical Inquiry, 7*(1), 213–36.

Thomas, G. (2010). Doing case study: Abduction not induction, phronesis not theory. *Qualitative Inquiry, 16*(7), 575–82.

van Dijk, T. A. (1975). Action, action description, and narrative. *New Literacy History, 6*(2), 273–94.

van Manen, M. (1990). *Researching lived experience: Human science for an active sensitive pedagogy.* Albany, NY: State University of New York Press.

Wallace, R. J., 'Practical Reason', The Stanford Encyclopedia of Philosophy (Summer 2009 edn.), Edward N. Zalta (Ed.), <http://plato.stanford.edu/archives/sum2009/entries/practical-reason/> accessed January 31, 2015.

Watson, C. (2011). Staking a small claim for fictional narratives in social and educational research. *Qualitative Research, 11*(4), 395–408.

White, H. (1992). 'Historical emplotment and the problem of truth.' In S. Friedländer (Ed.), *Probing the limits of representation: Nazism and the "final solution"* (pp. 37–53). Cambridge, MA: Harvard University Press.

White, H. (2001). 'The historical text as literary artifact.' In G. Roberts (Ed.), *The history and narrative reader* (pp. 221–36). London: Routledge.

Whitebrook, M. (2001). *Identity, narrative and politics.* London: Routledge.

4

DIALECTICAL THINKING

The truth is . . . that the oppressed are not "marginals," are not people living "outside" society. They have always been "inside"—inside the structure which made them "beings for others." The solution is not to "integrate" them into the structure of oppression, but to transform that structure so that they can become "beings for themselves."

Paulo Freire, 1993, p. 55

The systematic erasure of all given unities enables us first of all to restore to the statement the specificity of its occurrence, and to show that discontinuity is one of those great accidents that create cracks not only in the geology of history, but also in the simple fact of the statement; it emerges in its historical irruption; what we try to examine is the incision that it makes, that irreducible—and very often tiny—emergence.

Michel Foucault, 1972a, p. 28

Introduction to Dialectical Thinking

Dialectical thinking is a form of relational thinking oriented toward change. It builds from categorical and narrative thinking, rejecting the aim of both to move human inquiry towards transformative action. Dialectical thinking challenges the objectification and essentialism associated with categorical thinking as well as the intentional and uniform view of the actor often portrayed in narrative thinking. Researchers using dialectical approaches believe that there are problems in the way things are which need to be surmounted and that focusing on understanding these problems is insufficient. What is needed is a way to change the problematic social arrangement. A core assumption guiding approaches considered to be "dialectic" is that human consciousness, personal identity, cultural norms and beliefs, and so on, cannot be understood apart from the historical, structural, and material conditions of which they are an integral part. Furthermore, "at the heart of dialectics is the idea that all 'things' are actually processes, that these processes are in constant motion, or development, and that this development is driven by the tension created by two interrelated opposites acting in contradiction with each other" (Au, 2007, p. 177). A concern, then, for researchers working in the dialectical mode of thinking is how best to enter this continuous movement in order to effect change in a desirable way.

The two quotes introducing this chapter were purposefully chosen to illustrate two very different ways of thinking that dialectics has generated for the social sciences. The first, which philosopher Seyla Benhabib (1986) calls "the politics of fulfillment," wholeheartedly embraces dialectical thinking and works from within conflicting entities to effect desired change. The second, which Benhabib calls "the politics of transfiguration," acknowledges the powerful effects of dialectics but works against it, seeking instead to break it apart, disrupting its constitutive power and internal movement. As will be evident from the characteristics of dialectical thinking listed later, research drawing on dialectical thinking puts into practice a wide variety of approaches, using one or both of these orientations in distinctive ways. In Benhabib's words:

> The politics of fulfillment envisages that the society of the future attains more adequately what present society has left unaccomplished. It is the culmination of the implicit logic of the present. The politics of transfiguration emphasizes the emergence of qualitatively new needs, social relations, and modes of association, which burst open the utopian potential within the old.
>
> *Benhabib, 1986, p. 13*

Benhabib believes that any research seeking to benefit from what has been opened by dialectics must take into account both orientations; a challenge that continues to inspire social researchers seeking to put into action subversive aims for the social sciences.

What connects these two very different orientations is a move away from a social science oriented to understanding what is going on in society, to one that views society, its norms, discourses, and practices, as a problem needing to be reformed. Research is now conceived of as an intervention, a political, and transformative act that works with, and for, *praxis* conceived of as "the self-creative activity through which we make the world" (Lather, 1991, p. 11). A problem for researchers seeking to effect change is that dialectical strategies have been conceptualized as both, like Freire's introductory quote suggests, the necessary part of all transformative action, and, as Foucault's quote suggests, a powerful movement that must itself be broken open if transformation is to occur. Part of the reason that both perspectives need to be presented together is that their different orientations and aims "are often conflated and confused" (Levinson, 1995, p. 113). Most often, it seems, the conflation occurs when theories of transfiguration get taken up to provide support for theories of fulfillment, even though the two orientations are conceptually quite distinct. For example, in Chapter 3 on narrative thinking, Lisa was introduced through one of her stories. In actuality, the primary mode of thinking employed in my dissertation study on parental involvement was dialectical. Although I collected many narratives from parents this was not in order to understand their individual experiences of involvement. Rather, I assumed that how parents talked about involvement would provide a window into the broad discourse of involvement that I believed circulated through a complex network of systems of meaning, whether or not these represented parents' actual experiences. I believed that dialectical thinking provided a way for me to theorize the continuous movement of a discourse like parental involvement, or a grouping like social class, "independently of the intentions of their individual members, who nonetheless benefitted from (or suffered) the consequences" (Teira, 2011, p. 83). In the analysis of Lisa's and other parents' accounts, I was interested, and provided evidence for, the way in which one's class location intersected with the parental involvement discourse, ultimately participating in the maintenance of an unequal system for parents and their children. After analyzing the parent narratives in order to help me understand the parents' experiences and the way their social class positions seemed to shape those experiences, I considered "the central role discourse itself plays in the creation and maintenance of social positions and relations" (Freeman, 2001a, p. 205). Drawing upon philosopher Michel Foucault's (1980) analysis of the intersection of power and knowledge, I concluded that the parental involvement discourse maintained inequalities in education and society in at least two interconnected ways. The first was that it had never functioned as a partnership with parents but, instead, reinforced a narrow view of the "good" parent from which all parents' actions were measured. Second, parental involvement practices gave the false impression that power was being shared with parents, but this was an illusion that not only served institutions by maintaining the status quo, but transferred the responsibility for success or failure onto the individual. I drew support for this finding from Foucault (1980) who wrote: "The individual . . . is not the *vis-à-vis* of power, it is . . . one of its prime effects" (p. 98). Foucault's philosophy of power provided support for my critique of parental involvement policies and practices, as well as a way to imagine their re-articulation. This is because, in a dialectical view of the world, humans and structures are believed to be in a constituting–constitutive relationship, so change can only occur by reconceptualizing that relationship.

What I did not understand at the time was that I was reading Foucault through Freire's radical democratic humanism (Aronowitz, 1993) without really understanding Foucault's relation to, and departure from, a subject-centered position (Foucault, 1977). I was unable to understand that the individual he was speaking of does not exist in the way I was conceptualizing him or her. Although, I understood that the individuals in my study were constructed within systems of oppression, I believed that their collective action was necessary to confront and reconstruct these systems from within. In contrast, the individual that Foucault was referring to is a concept formed at the intersections of multiple overlapping relations of power, a way of perceiving power as an emergent force that has influenced the development of diagrammatical modes of thinking (Deleuze, 1988) which are described in Chapter 6. However, poststructural theorists such as Foucault have contributed enormously to the conversation about the potentials and limits of dialectical thinking, and their work supports a large body of research working both within, and against, dialectics. The reason for this is that dialectics itself provides the ground for this move. It does this by embodying a "logic of freedom" (Bhaskar, 1993, p. 374). As philosopher Roy Bhaskar explains: "The dialectic is a flexible instrument. . . . [It is] neither good nor bad in itself, except insofar as it empowers us in our understanding and transformation of reality" (p. 374).

Freedom, from a dialectical perspective, is *praxis*, in that it lies in the trans-formational possibilities opened up by the dialectical movement itself; possibilities that always exceed the constitutive material present in any historical moment (Hoffmeyer, 1994). For fulfillment-oriented dialectical researchers freedom is not a given but must be pursued: "Freedom is not an ideal located outside of man. . . . It is rather the indispensable condition for the quest for human completion" (Freire, 1993, p. 29). From this perspective humans and the world are always "beings in the process of *becoming*" (Freire, 1993, p. 65), but this becoming needs to be nurtured if humans are to co-construct a world in which they can be more fully themselves. However, "the possibility of constant change" (Rajchman, 1985, p. 123) opened up by dialectics also provides the ground for a non-dialectical freedom. Such a freedom "is found in dissolving or changing the politics that embody our nature, and as such it is asocial or anarchical" (Rajchman, 1985, p. 123). Emancipation from a transfigurative perspective "signifies a radical and qualitative break with some aspects of the present" (Benhabib, 1986, pp. 41–2) and requires "reeducation and transformation, the objects of needs and pleasures would be redefined" (Benhabib, 1986, p. 113). As I will illustrate in the section on dialectical thinking in practice, one of the ways this reeducation has been conceptualized is by rewriting history and making visible an alternative history; one that has been hidden or distorted by the workings of power (Foucault, 1972a). Understanding the characteristics of dialectical thinking, therefore, is crucial to understanding theories and methodologies seeking ways to work with and/ or against dialectics to effect change.

Characteristics of Dialectical Thinking

Dialectical thinking is so ingrained in our societal structures and modes of being that, like categorical and narrative thinking, its presentation usually brings forth recognition from the audience, rather than surprise. As Maxine Greene (1988) explains: "There is . . . a dialectical relation marking every human situation: the relation between subject and object, individual and environment, self and society, outsider and community, living consciousness and phenomenal world" (p. 8). As a theory of change, dialectical thinking has played a dominant role in explaining historical and social changes, as well as the continuous changes occurring in the natural world (Engels, 1940; Gould, 2002). So even though there are many "dialectics" (see Bhaskar, 1993; Rescher, 2007), as theories of change, they exhibit certain shared characteristics.

   1. *Everything is interconnected and made up of dynamic intersecting parts.* Dialectical theorists view the world as a network of colliding and competing forces that cannot avoid coming into contact with one another. As political theorist Friedrich Engels posited:

> The whole of nature accessible to us forms a system, an interconnected totality of bodies, and by bodies we understand here all material existence extending from stars to atoms, indeed right to ether particles, in so far as one grants the existence of the last named.
>
> *Engels, 1940, p. 36*

A key concern, therefore, for dialectical researchers is how to understand what is meant by "system" and the role each part plays in creating and maintaining such a system, including the role and effects of the research situation itself. How natural scientists have dealt with this issue is beyond the scope of this book; for social scientists, however, working with this issue is one of the determining factors of dialectical research.

   One way theorists have addressed this is by speculating that all systems "gain their identity through their parts, and . . . parts come into being through wholes" (Roberts, 2014, p. 20). Social scientists working with dialectical strategies must therefore not only identify the system(s) of influence they feel matter to their study and who should be included in their target population, they must also determine how they will theorize the relationship between the two. For example, in the late 1970s, feminist researcher Bonnie Dill (1979) proposed "a dialectical framework to analyze the condition of black women in the family . . . [based on] a conviction that the relationship of blacks to white society is dialectical in nature" (p. 546). She theorized that the relationship black women have with white society is multi-dimensional and complex, and not likely to be the same for all black women, or for any woman as she participated in a variety of situations. Because all "wholes" gain their identity from their parts, the whole in question in dialectical research is a whole constructed at the intersection of parts identified for the purpose of the study. In Dill's study, these parts—race relations in general, women's roles in the family, women's work, and so on—made up the social context within which the experiences of the black women could be understood. The complexity of these intersecting systems, including the individual nature of each woman, accounts for the variety that Dill sought to uncover and understand. Dialectical researchers, therefore, do not believe organisms act alone, or that the capacity for change resides solely in the organism itself, but is always the result of complex intersecting forces.

2. *Change is inevitable and is the result of friction within, and between, living and nonliving organisms.* "The root idea of dialectic lies in the Heraclitean conception of an oscillation between opposing forces in a productive tension where each turning makes a constructive contribution to the effective functioning of the overall process" (Rescher, 2007, p. 120). Although there are various interpretations of what Heraclitus may have meant about flux and the role played by opposing forces[1] (Graham, 2015), a key concept for dialectical thinking is that of friction, which results when oppositional forces come into contact with one another. Friction, however, is not the result of simple dichotomies, but of complex, intersecting entities seeking stability.

> Dialectical thinking thrives on the awareness of contradictions. But it also goes much further: Dialectical thinking encourages the unearthing of hidden or tacit contradictions. It does not "accept" or "tolerate" contradictions; rather, it seeks to resolve contradictions, leading to higher levels of understanding.
>
> *Ho, 2000, p. 1065*

Although dialectical thinking is based on the idea that everything has an opposite (Wan, 2012), it is important to understand that the tensions depicted by dialectics should not be reduced to simple oppositions or contradictions (Bhaskar, 1993), but include multiple, often undefined, intersecting contradictory elements. Another assumption guiding dialectics therefore is that change resulting from dialectical friction is inevitable because systems do not tolerate instability: "The driving mechanism of dialectic is instability—be it the instability of thought (most drastically exemplified by self-contradiction) or the instability of condition typified by the vagaries of nature or the fickleness of man" (Rescher, 2007, p. 5). Change, therefore, is believed to be a movement towards stability, in whatever form that might take.

Psychologist Michael Basseches (2005) examined the dialectical analysis of both Marx's history of production and Kuhn's history of science. He explained how they both characterize the way social practices are shaped by, as well as shape, those involved in the practice, and the way those involved threaten stability. Since tensions are believed to be inherent within individuals and systems as well as between them, a dominant social practice is always at risk of being overthrown from within. As Basseches explained, when enough tensions or anomalies are produced in ways that the current formation cannot resolve, a new formation is bound to be created. And along with new formations are new rules of practice. Nevertheless, even though dialectics is often presented in cyclical terms, as the next point shows, the aim of dialectical thinking for research is rarely synthesis; that is, the aim is not to eliminate the world of difference, but to find more socially just ways to account for, and include, different perspectives within the dialectical movement (Lather, 1986), as the fourth point illustrates.

3. *The movement of change is cyclical and continuous.* Philosopher Nicholas Rescher (2007, p. 1) depicts the phases believed to occur in a continuous dialectical process:

- *Initiation* (positing, declaration, inauguration)
- *Response* (counter-reaction, reply, opposition, destabilization)
- *Revision and readjustment* (operational modification, sophistication, complexification)

Figure 4.1 depicts this dialectical movement.

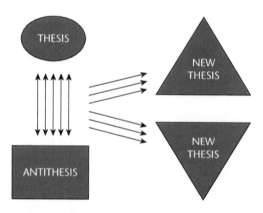

FIGURE 4.1 Dialectical Friction and Emergence

The social world, then, is believed to be the product of "a temporal flow of determining and determined contradictory phenomena continuously emerging from a potential state to become realised and going back to a potential state" (Carchedi, 2009, p. 147). This does not mean, however, that change can be accurately traced. There are disagreements about whether to conceptualize change as a continuous or discontinuous process. For example, in his presentation of Marx's dialectical method, philosopher Philip Kain writes:

The structure of categories with which we understand an historical epoch in which one form of production predominates will not lead to an understanding of the structure of categories relevant to the comprehension of a succeeding epoch in which a different form of production predominates.

Kain, 1980, pp. 299–300

This point poses new problems for dialectical thinkers. If everything is an outcome of complex negotiations between contradictions, and this outcome actually replaces the old (Wan, 2012), then describing change is not easy. Furthermore, since "the driving force of a dialectical process is the destabilization or discord issuing from the counter-reaction against an initial state of things that is an already achieved given" (Rescher, 2007, p. 5), then discord is not only inevitable if change is left to "nature," but required, if change is desired. These ongoing dynamic interactions between "naturally-occurring" forces and human-initiated interventions make dialectical research not only challenging, but are one reason for the diversity in designs and orientations. The reason for the quote marks around naturally-occurring is that for many dialectical researchers, naturally-occurring forces include the numerous socially-constructed arrangements that are so deeply ingrained that they seem natural. A point philosopher Emmanuel Eze makes about the concept of race:

Questions about reason and human identity, including racial identity, have always clung together in modern thought, so that the dialectical movements of thought which organize the world, including our racial consciousness, present race to us as itself a domain of the rational.

Eze, 2001, p. 41

Seeking a postracial future, Eze takes readers into a dialectical analysis of the historical, cultural, linguistic, experiential, economic, and philosophical manifestations of race to reveal, critique, and consider this socially constructed part of our social world. His analysis reveals how difference is deeply ingrained in all cultural practices, including language. Words like "black" and "white" have complex, historical and prejudicial meanings and associated values that cannot be ignored when considering human experience.

To transcend race in the ways I think of it is therefore not an invitation to the oppressed to abandon resistance to racism, but rather a suggestion that this resistance must also be seen to include efforts to overcome the master narrative of race itself. It is to imagine a future when no one is forced into a position in which one must automatically bear the privileges or the costs of a racial tag.

Eze, 2001, p. 223

Describing the dialectical process as a "movement through forms," Basseches (2005) states: "The definition of dialectic relies upon and presupposes both the notion of movement and the notion of form and focuses on a particular relationship between them" (p. 50). Therefore, overcoming "the master narrative" as Eze suggests requires both an understanding of how such narratives get constructed, as well as how they move through systems of meaning dispersing their effects along the way.

4. *Dialectical thinking works with, and against, the dialectical movement of change.* A crucial problem for dialectical thinkers is how to work with multiple constitutive transformational relationships in a way that overcomes the inherent limitation of dialectics. This is because, like categorical thinking, identification of the concepts believed to be constructing "the way things are" risks reinforcing their presence and power rather than producing the desired change. As Eze's quote about transcending race suggests, resistance alone is insufficient. It must also involve critique and disruption of the systems of meaning that give shape to the relations between concepts. How this critique is conceptualized is one of the defining features of dialectical thinking, while also being the transformative movement that differentiates one dialectical approach from another, as illustrated in the next section.

Dialectics is inherently critical because it must bring together differing or opposing perspectives or forces—the "negative" of a "positive"—in order to construct something new. Raphael Foshay (2002) explains: "Negation, the negative, is *the* dialectical notion *per se*, because, unlike its opposite, the positive, it is quintessentially relational, not to say inherently dependent" (p. 296). However, the relationship between a positive and a negative always plays a transformative role that threatens to alter the role of the negative from one of causing important friction to being one and the same dimensionally as the positive it is meant to oppose. Negation, then, becomes defined by this paradoxical "character as a nothing that in some way exists, that only exists in, as, and through contradiction" (Foshay, 2002, p. 296). A problem for dialectical researchers is that the very process of working its transformational potential involves identification and synthesis of its constitutive, and interdependent, parts; a process that threatens to reduce and turn the needed dynamic movement into something static. To overcome this issue has necessitated a different kind of negation, such as philosopher Theodor Adorno's "negative" dialectics. Adorno explains:

> To this end, dialectics is obliged to make a final move: being at once the impression and the critique of the universal delusive context, it must now turn even against itself. The critique of every self-absolutizing particular is a critique of the shadow which absoluteness casts upon the critique; it is a critique of the fact that critique itself, contrary to its own tendency, must remain within the medium of the concept. It destroys the claim of

identity by testing and honoring it; therefore, it can reach no farther than that claim. The claim is a magic circle that stamps critique with the appearance of absolute knowledge. It is up to the self-reflection of critique to extinguish that claim, to extinguish it in the very negation of negation that will not become a positing.

Adorno, 1973, p. 406

Negative dialectics works with the movement of dialectics against itself by continuously dispersing the emerging new constructions. "Negative dialectics is the unending transformation of concepts into their opposites, of what is into what could be but is not" (Benhabib, 1986, p. 173). In other words, dialectical thinking involves working *with* dialectics by actively engaging with the friction generated when a thesis is brought into relation with a counter-thesis, and *against* dialectics, by finding ways to continuously defer or suspend closure, or a final synthesis. As will be evident in the next section, for social scientists, this work must take into account the dynamic and ambiguous nature of language itself: "What negative dialectic makes us aware of is something our use of language as a tool for communication, or a medium for transferring contents, makes us forget. It is the potential of language to disclose experience through its expressive moment" (Foster, 2007, p. 199). In other words, dialectical researchers take seriously the so-called linguistic turn, which asserts that all philosophical problems are problems of language (see Rorty, 1992, for an interesting collection of essays about this issue). As the examples in the next section illustrate, dialectical researchers have also taken seriously the experiential and transformative potential of language, turning this potential back on itself in the form of critical and generative dialogic encounters (Freire, 1993), or discursively by retracing the evidence and effect of the co-construction between historical conditions, knowledge and power, and the meaning-making systems shaping human self-understanding (Foucault, 1972a).

Finally, what is important to understand about this complex movement is that dialectics is an emergentist theory (Wan, 2012). "By its very nature, the synthesis is a novel construction that departs from both the thesis and antithesis" (Van de Ven & Poole, 1995). Recall Foucault's quote introducing this chapter. Since the synthesis emerging from the friction between a thesis and a counter-thesis actually replaces (negates) these entities, the chain of events, or history, can only be hypothesized. As an emergentist theory, therefore, dialectical thinking has a complex relationship with the social sciences and has had a much broader influence than can be addressed here. For example, it has played a central role in conversations about the nature of time and change, order and disorder, reversibility and irreversibility, and so on (Burger, Cohen, & DeGrood, 1980). And these issues in turn have influenced how social scientists have made use of the generative process offered by dialectics. In general, dialectical researchers have theorized ways to work *with* the dialectical movement believed to be created through friction, and *with* some process for making visible the entities believed to be in friction. As illustrated in the next section, this work is built on the idea that a better understanding of the interdependence between constitutive structures, practices, discourses, and so on, and the impacted beliefs, understandings, social arrangements, and so on, will provide the necessary ground for reconstructing constitutive relationships or problematic arrangements. However, as I point out in the final section of this chapter, the idea of emergence has been taken beyond dialectics and influenced the development of poetical and diagrammatical thinking, the topics of Chapters 5 and 6.

Dialectical Thinking in Practice

The relationship between individuals and society encompasses many levels of dialectical tension making the inclusion of some form of dialectical thinking probable in all inquiry. Simply recognizing that the movement of analysis involves working across diverse perspectives or that language itself is dialogic (Bakhtin, 1986) opens a dialectical space for inquiry. Furthermore, since competing forces can be internal or external to the organism or entity being inquired about or, most likely, involve both, the magnitude of research designs employing dialectical strategies is endless. As Wan explains, dialectical thinking can

> serve certain heuristic purposes by highlighting, for example, emergence, complexity, historicity, dynamic change, contingency, the interweaving of continuity and discontinuity, the interpenetration of seemingly mutually exclusive categories, the relative autonomy of different levels of matter in motion, and so on.
>
> *Wan, 2012, p. 438*

Two central concerns, however, bring social science researchers working in the dialectical mode together. The first is a concern for how to account for, and address, difference in social science research. Since difference is perceived to be a fundamental part of all social life, and the various forms it takes produce a multiplicity of effects, social scientists interested in change have wondered how to best work with difference to effect change in desirable ways. The second is the belief that inquiry should play a transformative role in society and an emancipatory role for individuals oppressed by current and/or past social arrangements. Furthermore, inherent to taking an approach that works within these tensions is the recognition that research is never neutral or innocent and always participates, for better or worse, in the changing landscape. In keeping with the two introductory quotes to this chapter, I have divided the practice section into two general orientations to research: one which is dialogue-centered, the other discourse-centered. Although both approaches can be, and have been, used together, separating them helps to describe how each makes use of dialectical thinking in their design. Furthermore, as mentioned in the introductory chapter, this distinction provides support for how I have conceptualized the two modes of thinking described in the next two chapters.

In general, both the dialogue- and discourse-oriented approaches work from the assumption that there is a co-constitutive relationship between the social or natural world and human consciousness or understanding (Au, 2007), and that research must somehow account for that constitutive relationship. They differ, however, in their point of entry into this dialectical relationship. The first approach is human-centered, participatory, "action-oriented [and] . . . forward-looking rather than simply reporting on the status quo" (Mitchell, DeLange, Moletsane, Stuart, & Buthelezi, 2005, p. 268). It aims to disrupt the objectification of the human, and works with subjective meaning-making to reconstruct more humane relationships. Although it is understood that humans enter a world that has already been named and constructed in particular ways, the focus is on how humans make sense of that world and their efforts to change it. The second is discourse-centered and conceptual, and is built on the assumption that all discourses and practices have material effects, and shape how humans understand themselves and others. It is historical and seeks transformation by revealing the way taken-for-granted conceptualizations of reality (the categories, narratives, and social arrangements that shape the world) are illusions constructed at the intersection of multiple, competing discourses. Rather than prioritize dialogue with humans, researchers enter the flow of competing discourse and focus on the ways these discourses have shaped the world. Table 4.1 outlines these two approaches.

TABLE 4.1 Two Approaches to Dialectical Thinking in Practice

	Dialogue-Centered Approach	*Discourse-Centered Approach*
Dialectical Action	Dialogue with Difference	Tracing Competing Concept Formations
Point of Entry into Dialectical Relationship	Human Experiences and Concerns	Language, Concepts, Material Practices
Nature of Analysis	Future and Action-Oriented	Historical and Reconstructive-Oriented

Although, there is no "road map to follow" (Jorgensen, 2005, p. 30), the examples in this section provide a brief overview of what these two approaches might look like in practice.

Dialogue-Centered Dialectical Research

To exist, humanly, is to *name* the world, to change it. Once named, the world in its turn reappears to the namers as a problem and requires of them a new *naming*. Human beings are not built in silence, but in word, in work, in action-reflection.

Paulo Freire, 1993, p. 69

Dialogue, for theorists like Freire, provides a way for human agents to enter into the dialectical process of naming and renaming the world. It is only through dialogue that humans can achieve a "consciousness *of* consciousness" (Freire, 1974, p. 107, as quoted in Au, 2007, p. 178), which helps them step outside their situation and begin the process of reconceptualizing a situation from one of limit to one of possibility. Since human cognitive shifts are believed to happen in situations where an opposite force produces tension, dialectical approaches seek to create the conditions to enact a dialogue with difference, and achieve a critical "co-understanding" (Cohen-Cruz, 2006, p. 433)—a necessary precursor to transformative action. It is only by dialoguing with others who have different experiences with current social arrangements and relationships, and different conceptions of how things could be, that humans can begin to transform these relationships and construct more socially-just arrangements. In this approach, different perspectives are sought out, especially those of people believed to have been marginalized, oppressed, or silenced by dominant social norms and practices (Collins, 2009). Caroline New (1998) explains: "Subjugated knowledges can be key to social change, not because they are the whole truth, but because they include information and ways of thinking which dominant groups have a vested interest in suppressing" (p. 360). Furthermore, since these knowledges are partial and overlap, they provide a source of experiential evidence for building solidarity and engaging in collective action (New, 1998). Dialogue provides the dialectically induced generative space to unpack, reflect upon, criticize, and reconsider the variety of opinions offered on an issue. The learning and understanding produced through dialogue is believed to be as, if not more, important, than the hoped-for solution to a problem (Jorgensen, 2005). The aim of entering the flow of change and keeping the conversation open, so to speak, is to play a significant role in shaping the resulting construction.

A core challenge for enacting dialogue-centered approaches is that the research situation itself is understood as a system that produces both desirable and undesirable effects. So researchers working in a dialectical mode believe that they must always position their research within the very tensions they are seeking to understand and change. Critical educator Michelle Fine called this stance "working the hyphens":

When we opt . . . simply to write *about* those who have been Othered, we deny the hyphen. . . . When we opt, instead, to engage in social struggles *with* those who have been exploited and subjugated, we work the hyphen, revealing far more about ourselves, and far more about the structures of Othering.

Fine, 1994, p. 72

Therefore, dialogue for critical action should be understood dialectically as a performative space where difference is articulated in ways that do not seek fusion but a re-drawing of the hyphen. Ethnographer Dwight Conquergood (1985) describes this performative stance as a space where diverse perspectives are brought into conversation in order to learn from, and challenge, one another. The aim is to engage *in* an open conversation that "resists conclusions . . . [and works] the space *between* competing ideologies. It brings self and other together even while it holds them apart. It is more like a hyphen than a period" (p. 9). In other words, dialectical researchers seek to effect change by disrupting the arrangements categorical thinking might have established, and producing alternative narratives that problematize taken-for-granted beliefs about human action. Focusing on the tensions that result at the intersections of societal arrangements and individuals is meant to go beyond simple empathy for others and incite collective action (Conquergood, 1985; Freire, 1993; Madison, 2011).

However, since one of the core assumptions guiding dialectical work is that no one can speak for another, and that change must occur from within each of us in the process of coming to an understanding, the challenge for dialectical researchers has been how to engage with others in ways that support everyone's critical transformative capacities without imposing a particular transformative process or outcome. Although a core idea is to open up a "space for groups to take action themselves . . . and come up with their own creative solutions" (Mitchell et al., 2005, p. 268), there are disagreements about who should be involved in those groups. Most groups, whether considered homogeneous or heterogeneous, will often bring together a range of differences, and so a common belief for participatory researchers is that participatory research approaches cannot, in and of themselves, alleviate concerns about power, rather they must seek to address these head-on. Revolutionary themes of "justice, equality, civil rights, [and] democracy" (Benhabib, 1986, p. 13) often guide this process.

Dialogue-centered approaches seeking collective action can take many forms. One common approach is to seek out the perspectives of groups of people typically excluded from decision-making processes as important contributors to transforming practice. Anna Ziersch, Gilbert Gallaher, Fran Baum, and Michael Bentley's (2011) study on the health inequities of Australian Aboriginal people examined "how Aboriginal people living in Adelaide make sense of, and respond to, experiences of racism and, in so doing, examines its implication for Aboriginal peoples' health and wellbeing" (p. 1045). Although they concluded that it is important to seek ways to "promote health-protective responses to racism" (p. 1045) for Aboriginal people, in line with dialectical thinking they provided no clear unifying set of guidelines to be adopted by all. Rather they argued that any response or reaction could be considered harmful or beneficial for all involved and suggested a continued need for more research into anti-racist practices in health.

Another common strategy for dialogue-centered dialectical research is to use the study as a form of intervention to foster the educational qualities of critical dialogue for participants themselves. For example, Rita Kohli's (2012) study of teacher interracial dialogue used dialectical thinking as a form of engagement meant to support collective understanding and the development of transformative action. As a critical race theorist, the conceptualization for her study came when she attended a teacher professional development workshop at a middle school on the subject of racial fights among students, and realized that "many teachers at the school had deep-rooted stereotypes and misconceptions about other races" (p. 181). Kohli surmised that the teachers' inability to recognize the common features of their own oppression would make it difficult for them to work with each other and with students in their search for a way to prevent further fighting. Her study sought, therefore, to help teachers of color develop a deeper awareness of the way systematic occurrences and experiences with racism affected all people of color. Kohli, a South Asian American woman and former teacher, felt she was in a good position to facilitate a critical dialogue on this topic with her participants—"12 black, Latina, and Asian American women enrolled in a teacher education program" (p. 182)—as a way to develop a deeper understanding of the "manifestation of racism in communities outside their own" (p. 186).

Dialectical thinking guided the design of the study, the prompts for the conversations, and the analysis, which sought to bring out the underlying structures that provided contexts for the teachers' "individual experiences with race and racism" as well as ways to reflect on and discuss "manifestations of oppression across race and culture" (Kohli, 2012, p. 191). Scheduling three focus groups with the student teachers helped Kohli create the time and space needed for the women to share their experiences, analyze and compare the similarities and differences of these experiences, and develop strategies to address racism in their schools. Kohli described how critical interracial dialogue created the catalyst for developing an awareness of racism as a social phenomenon beyond the student teachers' individual experiences and an understanding of the ways diverse beliefs, languages, religions, and other cultural practices affected these experiences. Working together to develop strategies to address racism within diverse classrooms fostered cultural competencies that would hopefully transform teacher action and benefit students. The resulting collective action did not necessarily mean that everyone believed the same thing or agreed with the same course of action, but it did suggest that there was a willingness to reach beyond one's own pre-understandings and work with others who may have a different idea of the world. As Greene (1988) explains:

"Multiple interpretations constitute multiple realities; the 'common' itself becomes multiplex and endlessly challenging, as each person reaches out from his/her own ground toward what might be, should be, is not yet" (p. 21).

Finally, another common approach is to work with participants themselves in the design and analysis of research meant to transform their lives. Yasser Payne and Hanaa Hamdi (2009) demonstrate the importance of participatory action research as a way to rethink intervention from something done to people to a way of working "with the men inside their community" (p. 30). Working with four American-born African men from Paterson, New Jersey, they examined "men's system of bonding with each other and the local community" (p. 30), especially in regards to their perceptions and experiences of street life. Prior to conducting the study all members of the participatory action research team—the four men and two lead researchers—underwent in-depth training involving "exercises centered on theory, method and analysis" (p. 36). The research itself consisted of interviews, focus groups, surveys, the mapping of "street communities of interest" (p. 36), and several rounds of analysis. All members of the team participated in the data collection and analysis.

Payne and Hamdi's approach simultaneously disrupted multiple taken-for-granted perspectives by conceptualizing the street as a site of resilience and humanity, and by incorporating the "phenomenological framing of the men's personal and social experiences with family, friends and other residents of the local community" (p. 44) in ways that revealed how much they cared about the welfare of their community and families. Dialectical thinking guided the analysis of this study by reframing traditional binaries, such as criminality versus morality, and theorizing these from a "both/and" perspective in order to problematize the prevailing belief that a person's criminal activity determined their level of care, or their commitment to the betterment of their lives and neighborhoods (Payne & Hamdi, 2009).

Discourse-Centered Dialectical Research

In every society the production of discourse is at once controlled, selected, organized and redistributed by a certain number of procedures whose role is to ward off its powers and dangers, to gain mastery over its chance events, to evade its ponderous, formidable materiality.
Michel Foucault, 1984, p. 109

Discourse-centered researchers work with the idea that language is a meaning-making agent in its own right. Language conceived discursively "builds objects, worlds, minds and social relations. It doesn't just reflect them" (Wetherell, 2001, p. 16). James Gee explains:

[A discourse] is a "dance" that exists in the abstract as a coordinated pattern of words, deeds, values, beliefs, symbols, tools, objects, times, and places and is the here and now as a performance that is recognizable as just such a coordination.

Gee, 2014, p. 53

Therefore, discourse analysts focus on the co-constitutive "relationship between discourse and other elements of social practices" (Fairclough, 2003, p. 207), and the historical conditions that account for the processes in which systems of knowledge have penetrated and shaped everyday knowledge, beliefs, actions, and interactions. The aim of discourse analysis is to identify the "procedures" that construct discourse and obscure its distributive effects, and to articulate new relationships between discourses and practices in order to produce different effects. Understanding the products of our research "as a kind of fiction . . . means that we come to see 'truth' as something less final; as something we can (re)make" (Graham, 2011, p. 666).

Although discourses play a large role in human meaning-making they are believed to have a life of their own, and therefore cannot be connected to human intentions or actions in any consistent way. As such, a focus on discourse dissolves the distinction between structure and agent, viewing both as implicated in discourse formations themselves. Therefore, the task of analysis is not to understand what something means, but to examine "possible enunciations that could be made on a particular subject, why it is that certain statements emerged to the exclusion of all others and what function they serve" (Graham, 2011, p. 667). There are no predetermined methods to this kind of analysis. When taken up dialectically the analysis works with the tensions and contradictions embedded in competing discourses—linguistic, disciplinary, conceptual, and so on—in ways that reveal their workings, that is, how they produce certain meaning structures, while stifling others.

Celine-Marie Pascale's (2005) study of the way representations of homelessness and the homeless were portrayed discursively in newspaper articles is a good example of this approach. Pascale analyzed 413 news stories about homelessness appearing between 1982 and 1996 in three major newspapers to show how the concept of homelessness became a part of everyday discourse and how its meaning underwent many changes as it got tangled up with other economic, moral, and political discourses. Her aim was to examine the constitutive work of discourse itself in the construction of a social class like the homeless outside of the economic conditions themselves. The point here is not to retrace Pascale's analysis but to illustrate the contributions dialectical discourse analysis can make to social science research. Pascale's analysis revealed the material effects of language as it was taken up by multiple intersecting social discourses, and how these effects resulted in changes to the concept of homelessness in ways that did not necessarily benefit the homeless themselves. After providing an overview of the discursive trends in how the homeless were represented over time (for example, as "drifters . . . accustomed to life on the streets. . . .

[As] hardworking people who lost their homes because of structural economic changes. . . . [Or as] former mental patients" (pp. 253–6), to name a few), Pascale provided a more complex analysis of some of the effects produced by the shifting and intersecting discourses. She demonstrated how both the discursive contents and their forms produced particular results over time; how they created a division between the homeless, and those who are not, that resulted in a stripping away of a nation's sense of responsibility and caring towards this less fortunate group of people, as well as an increased enforcement of rules that denied the homeless the rights to public spaces, and even to the norms of citizenship. She showed the power of language, such as calling a diverse group of people "the homeless" in ways that obscured individuals' genders, ages, ethnicities, and unique circumstances, or the way using a term like "home-less" (rather than "house-less") created a link to discourses of belonging, and built a false relationship between ownership and citizenship in ways that gave license for the non-homeless to withhold empathy and turn their backs on the issue. Through this analysis she demonstrated how a society's discourse practices produced "the very conditions of alienation they purport to describe" (p. 263), and advocated for resistance in the form of "disidentification," a way of "rethinking and reconstructing discourses in ways that expose what the hegemonic discourse intended to conceal" (p. 263).

Discourse-centered approaches focus on the tensions between everyday speaking and doing and "salient political, economic, and cultural formations" (Luke, 1995/1996, p. 11) which are believed to constitute them. As a result, what is assembled through the analysis is the way language is taken up in systems of meaning; that is, the way discourse is implicated in the production of meaning and relations of power. As a dialectical-relational analysis (Fairclough, 2009) the focus is on the constitutive effects of competing and interacting discourses with the aim of conceptualizing new relationships between discourses and social practices.

Deciding on Dialectical Thinking for Analysis

Dialectical thinking has had a huge impact on the social, natural, and human sciences, and I feel that I can confidently state that no discipline remains untouched by it. Furthermore, it is clear that some form of dialectics is present in all research. Less widespread is its adoption as the primary research strategy employed. This is due largely to dialectical researchers being unapologetic about their ideological and political leanings and their desire to openly challenge the dominant view of scientific research as objective and neutral. Since it is possible to conduct critical research—that is, research that provides a critique of taken-for-granted norms, beliefs, or practices—from either a categorical or narrative approach, or both, why would you choose to prioritize dialectical strategies in your research?

One of the primary reasons researchers choose a dialectical approach is to overcome the limitations believed to be inherent in any research approach that assumes it can produce social change by providing an account of an event, group, or phenomenon from a space of supposed objectivity or neutrality. Since dialectical thinking in the social sciences has been heavily influenced by Karl Marx's dialectical materialism and this approach was meant to revolutionize, not simply reform (Gregory, 1977), inherent to this way of thinking is a radical disruption of the established order, and this includes beliefs about the aims of research itself. Dialectical researchers believe that a critical social science must always refashion itself in response to "changing historical conditions" (Lather, 1991, p. 3). Furthermore, researchers drawing from dialectical approaches assume that change cannot be brought about without considerable struggle and that there is always risk with any process. Since all research has effect, the desire is for those effects to be beneficial to those affected, rather than otherwise. Greg Dimitriadis explains:

> Acknowledging culture as dialogic, as emergent, makes us responsible for the ways we as unique individuals inhabit one another's worlds, as well as how we write up our empirical material (or "data"), opening a space to see ethnography, writ large, as a political praxis . . . with real effects.
>
> *Dimitriadis, 2001, p. 579*

Therefore, dialectical approaches require a heightened sense of reflexivity and acknowledgment of the ideological values researchers draw upon and put into practice. Lather (1986) explains: "Dialectical practices require an interactive approach to research that invites reciprocal reflexivity and critique, both of which guard against the central dangers to praxis-oriented empirical work: imposition and reification on the part of the researcher" (p. 265).

Dialectical thinking, therefore, is a useful strategy when the aim of research is not only to understand the coordinating and relational processes involved in the construction of oppressive structures and systems of meaning in society, but also to transform them. Dialectical thinking has provided the theoretical foundation for researchers to:

- Uncover the tensions and contradictions believed to be inherent in humans and society
- Put into action a theory of change that works with the generative space of dialectical friction
- Construct counter-stories meant to critique and overthrow oppressive practices

Dialectical researchers believe that all research, whether intended or not, participates in the construction of the reality it seeks to describe, explain, or overthrow (see Hacking, 1983). Since effects can be both positive or negative, or more often than not, both, the constitutive effects of research are one of the core concerns facing dialectical researchers. However, since change is believed to be inevitable—that is, change will result from no action just as well as from action—researchers believe they must do the best they can to intervene in ways that direct change beneficially. As Lather's quote above points out, it is this latter point that has posed the most problems for dialectical researchers—how to intervene in ways that cause the most benefit and the least harm to social groups oppressed and marginalized by current social arrangements, while at the same time not creating new forms of oppression for these groups or others. Therefore, as an intervention, dialectical research involves a wide spectrum of challenges, of which only a portion can be introduced here. Nevertheless, there are several decisions all dialectical researchers must make. These can be organized under two broad questions: How to conceptualize dialectical change, and how to intervene in its flow. These are addressed, in reverse order, below.

Intervening in the flow of change. An issue for dialectical researchers, regardless of whether they are conducting a dialogue-centered or discourse-centered study, is the difficulty in demonstrating "how large-scale social discourses are systematically (or, for that matter, unsystematically) manifest in everyday talk and writing in local sites" (Luke, 1995/1996, p. 11). This is because the dialectical tensions involved are not only complex, but continuously changing as they interact with one another, making identification of core issues or concepts a challenging task. What to prioritize and what direction to take becomes an ongoing concern for researchers who are being asked to simultaneously facilitate an open process and somehow direct its course. A tension exists then between identification of competing and conflicting forces and the desire to let the dialectical process lead the way.

The need to name the powers of oppression as they are being criticized and unpacked has led to dialectical approaches being criticized for contributing to the very representational issues they are trying to overcome. By seeking to disrupt the constitutive relationships between discourses, social arrangements, and people's perceptions of themselves and others, dialectical researchers have generally drawn on the resources available to them. That is, they have looked to history or current arrangements, working from within these conceptualizations in search of points of transformation. The issue with such an approach, according to critics such as Foucault (1972b), is that what is being conceptualized—that is the relationship of the subject to the discourses that constitute him or her—belong to "the same system of thought" (p. 12) making revolutionary change unlikely. In addition, critics of dialectics, such as Foucault, believe that there is too much emphasis on history as a continuity of effects and not enough attention given to the idea that history can be conceptualized discontinuously (Foucault, 1972b).

To address this criticism, dialectical researchers have tried to find ways to keep the concepts or topics of conversation in movement, whether it is within the movement of a generative dialogue (Freire, 1993), or in the oscillation between a specific text and the "order of discourse" that provides its structuring network (Fairclough, 2003, p. 3). They have also sought ways to juxtapose competing discourses so as to break open the taken-for-granted, and create new ways of speaking about and representing the world. In other words, researchers seek ways to approach the entire project dialectically, both trusting that the process itself will provide the needed insight about how to proceed and finding ways to bring in original material with which to provoke new insights.

Related to the question of how to intervene are issues of representation. Dialectical researchers are encouraged to suspend preconceived notions about their participants' experiences and perspectives, and about what constitutes a desired end point for the project. However, in order to uncover and openly criticize the "sources"—the traditions, assumptions, practices—that play a role in constructing and maintaining dominant views of reality and that shape people's collective understanding of themselves and others, these have to be brought out into the open. This requires that researchers open themselves up to being transformed from within, to making themselves vulnerable and believing in the transformative value of learning from others (Gadamer, 1989). Conquergood (1985) explains: "When we have true respect for the Difference of other cultures, then we grant them the potential for challenging our own culture" (p. 9).

However, while researchers might bring a stance of respect for difference, reality can be quite complex. People, researchers included, are multifaceted and participate in oppressing practices as well as having experienced oppression (Freire, 1993). There are likely then to be conflicting opinions about which issues are most important, and how to represent individual and group perspectives on these issues. For example in their study of working class lives, Michelle Fine and Lois Weis were keenly aware of the dilemma of representing individual perspectives that might themselves be disparaging of others. They explain:

> There are no easy answers to these dilemmas. In each of the chapters in this book, we have tried to contextualize the narratives as spoken within economic, social, and racial contexts so that no one narrator is left holding the bag for his/her demographic group, but indeed there are moments when, within the narratives, "others"—people of color, caseworkers, men, women, the neighbor next door—are portrayed in very disparaging ways. Then we are waged in the battle of *representation*. We work hard to figure out how to represent and contextualize our narrators, ourselves, and the people about whom they are ranting.
>
> Fine & Weis, 1998, p. 282

Since dialectical researchers believe "that not all strife is bad: some may result in new and better things" (Bunge, 2001, p. 40), another challenge for them is how to surmount the natural tendency for people to avoid conflict and view conflict as something needing to be overcome as quickly as possible. Learning to overcome tendencies to minimize conflict, resolve issues quickly, or ignore them altogether can be challenging. Embedded in this issue are concerns for how to "account for the wide variety of cultural traditions, ethnic groupings, linguistic communities, and religious beliefs in human society" (Todd, 2009, p. 51) without offending, oppressing, or misinterpreting their perspectives. These issues are directly implicated in how difference and change are conceptualized.

Conceptualizing change and emergence. There are wide variations in dialectical theories. Bhaskar (1993) explains: "The materialist diffraction makes possible distinctions between ontological, epistemological, relational, metacritical, conceptual, practical, ethical, etc. dialectics" (p. 377). Going back to the idea of freedom, Bhaskar helps us to understand that for him freedom does not mean the elimination of conflicting forces for as he explains, (and the chapter on categorical thinking demonstrated), "a material world without absences is physically impossible" (p. 379). Dialectics is "the pulse of freedom" (p. 385), he states, because to exist one must "possess the capacity for self-development" (p. 385). Ultimately then, as the characteristics listed earlier have shown, dialectics is about self-development.

Dialectics have brought to the forefront essential issues for qualitative researchers, and have produced a wide range of ways of revealing their fallibilities and of making transparent their beliefs and practices. However, there are no agreements about how to conceptualize self-development, change, critique, or what is meant by "dialogue across difference." These issues have generated a wide range of scholarly materials that provide good resources for researchers interested in dialectical approaches. The point here is to not take for granted what dialectics means, but to consider how to use dialectical theories to conceptualize your perspective on difference, the movement of change you believe your study is enacting, and how you see them working together to fulfill the aims of your project. For example, in an article entitled, *Can there be pluralism without conflict?*, educator Sharon Todd (2009) argues that the project of democracy is less about "recognition and dialogue," and more about "an unending project of dissent and contestation" (p. 51), which suggests, assuming you agree with her, a key role for some form of dialectical thinking.

Additionally, Todd (2009) argues for a move beyond conceiving of pluralism based solely on "social attributes or identities," towards one that also takes into account "the emergence of subjectivity itself as a being-with others" (p. 51). In making this argument, Todd puts us directly into one of the conceptual tensions opened up by dialectics: how to account both for the events and concepts believed to be creating the friction *and* the new, original entity emerging from that space. The dialectical process will take on a very different shape if conflicting events, or *difference*, are believed to exist prior to their interaction, and remain somehow, even though in a changed form, in the emerging entity— a continuous although changing formulation—versus a conception where difference is itself an outcome of the interaction. Sociologist Pierre Bourdieu (1998) explains this latter point well. He states that a concept such as distinction which is usually considered a manner of being that sets you apart from others, "is nothing other than *difference*, a gap, a distinctive feature, in short, a *relational* property existing only in and through its relation with other properties" (p. 6).

I believe these two perspectives on difference are different versions of Basseches' (2005) "movement through forms;" different ways to theorize the dynamic space in which conflicting entities are brought into relation with each other, what is being brought together, and what is emerging from this space. This movement looks very different if theorized as a continuous, developmental process, versus an emergent, haphazard one. In making a pitch for theorizing discontinuity, Foucault (1972b) explains that discontinuity is not necessarily about rupture. Rather, it "is a play of specific transformations different from one another (each one having its conditions, its rules, its level) and linked among themselves according to schemes of dependence" (p. 233).

Theorists working with and against dialectics have sought ways to describe these transformations and the conditions which bring them together. In contrast, researchers seeking ways to work outside dialectics are finding ways to work with the idea of movement without needing to identify what is involved in that movement; a sort of transformation without formation. As mentioned in the introductory chapter, the insights that have germinated from conversations about dialectical theories and practices have provided support for two very different, although not necessarily incompatible, approaches: the poetical (described in Chapter 5) and the diagrammatical (described in Chapter 6). Poetical thinking departs from, and extends, the dialogue-centered approaches described by moving from a dialectical view of the human-world relation to one where human bodies and world are living and felt extensions and entanglements of each other. Whereas, diagrammatical thinking departs from, and extends, the discourse-centered approaches described earlier by moving from a dialectical view of the subject-discourse relation to one where the focus of analysis is on the between-state of entangled entities—the links mentioned by Foucault— which suggest new ways to conceptualize their articulation and entanglement. One is deeply human and embodied, the other posthuman and materialist.

Note

1 Graham's (2015) encyclopedia entry on Heraclitus suggests that one possible reading about Heraclitus's notion of change is "not that all things are changing so that we cannot encounter them twice, but something much more subtle and profound. It is that some things stay the same only by changing. One kind of long-lasting material reality exists by virtue of constant turnover in its constituent matter" (n.p.).

References

Adorno, T. W. (1973). *Negative dialectics* (trans. by E. B. Ashton). New York, NY: The Seabury Press.

Aronowitz, S. (1993). 'Paulo Freire's radical democratic humanism.' In P. McLaren & P. Leonard (Eds.), *Paulo Freire: A critical encounter* (pp. 8–24). New York, NY: Routledge.

Au, W. (2007). Epistemology of the oppressed: The dialectics of Paulo Freire's theory of knowledge. *Journal for Critical Education Policy Studies, 5*(2). <www.jceps.com/index.php?pageID=article&articleID=100> accessed June 7, 2015.

Bakhtin, M. M. (1986). *Speech genres & other late essays* (trans. by Vern W. McGee). Austin, TX: University of Texas Press.

Basseches, M. (2005). The development of dialectical thinking as an approach to integration. *Integral Review, 1,* 47–63.

Benhabib, S. (1986). *Critique, norm, and utopia: A study of the foundations of critical theory.* New York, NY: Columbia University Press.

Bhaskar, R. (1993). *Dialectic: The pulse of freedom.* London, UK: Verso.

Bourdieu, P. (1998). *Practical reason: On the theory of action.* Stanford, CA: Stanford University Press.

Bunge, M. (2001). *Philosophy in crisis: The need for reconstruction.* Amherst, NY: Prometheus Books.

Burger, A. R., Cohen, H. R., & DeGrood, D. H. (1980). *Marxism, science, and the movement of history.* Amsterdam, The Netherlands: B. R. Grüner Publishing.

Carchedi, G. (2009). The fallacies of "new dialectics" and value-form theory. *Historical Materialism, 17*(1), 145–69.

Cohen-Cruz, J. (2006). 'The problem democracy is supposed to solve: The politics of community-based performance.' In D. S. Madison & J. Hamera (Eds.), *The Sage handbook of performance studies* (pp. 427–45). Thousand Oaks, CA: Sage.

Collins, P. H. (2009). *Black feminist thought: Knowledge, consciousness, and the politics of empowerment.* New York, NY: Routledge.

Conquergood, D. (1985). Performing as a moral act: Ethical dimensions of the ethnography of performance. *Literature in Performance, 5*(2), 1–13.

Deleuze, G. (1988). *Foucault* (edited and trans. by Seán Hand). Minneapolis, MN: University of Minnesota Press (originally published in French, 1986).

Dill, B. T. (1979). The dialectics of black womanhood. *Signs, 4*(3), 543–55.

Dimitriadis, G. (2001). Coming clean at the hyphen: Ethics and dialogue at a local community center. *Qualitative Inquiry, 7*(5), 578–97.

Engels, F. (1940). *Dialectics of nature* (edited and trans. by Clemens Dutt). New York, NY: International Publishers.

Eze, E. C. (2001). *Achieving our humanity: The idea of the postracial future.* New York, NY: Routledge.

Fairclough, N. (2003). *Analysing discourse: Textual analysis for social research.* New York, NY: Routledge.

Fairclough, N. (2009). 'A dialectical-relational approach to critical discourse analysis in social research.' In R. Wodak & M. Meyer (Eds.), *Methods of critical discourse analysis* (2nd edn., pp. 162–86). Thousand Oaks, CA: Sage.

Fine, M. (1994). 'Working the hyphens: Reinventing self and other in qualitative research.' In N. K. Denzin & Y. S. Lincoln (Eds.), *Handbook of qualitative research* (pp. 70–82). Thousand Oaks, CA: Sage.

Fine, M., & Weis, L. (1998). *The unknown city: Lives of poor and working-class young adults.* Boston, MA: Beacon Press.

Foshay, R. (2002). 'Tarrying with the negative': Bataille and Derrida's reading of negation in Hegel's *Phenomenology. Heythrop Journal, 43*(3), 295–310.

Foster, R. (2007). *Adorno: The recovery of experience.* Albany, NY: State University of New York Press.

Foucault, M. (1972a). *The archaeology of knowledge and the discourse on language* (trans. by A. M. Sheridan Smith). New York, NY: Pantheon Books.

Foucault, M. (1972b). History, discourse and discontinuity (trans. by A. M. Nazzaro). *Salmagundi, 20,* pp. 225–48.

Foucault, M. (1977). *Language, counter-memory, practice: Selected essays and interviews* (trans. by Donald F. Bouchard and Sherry Simon). Ithaca, NY: Cornell University Press.

Foucault, M. (1980). *Power/knowledge: Selected interviews and other writings, 1972–1977* (C. Gordon, Ed.). New York, NY: Pantheon Books.

Foucault, M. (1984). 'The order of discourse.' In M. Shapiro (Ed.), *Language and politics* (pp. 108–38). New York, NY: New York University Press.

Freeman, M. (2001a). *Rearticulating the birthright of participation: Three tales of parental involvement.* Unpublished doctoral dissertation, State University of New York, Albany.

Freire, P. (1993). *The pedagogy of the oppressed* (new revised edn., trans. by Myra Bergman Ramos). New York: Continuum (original work published 1970).

Gadamer, H.-G. (1989). *Truth and method* (2nd revised edn., trans. by J. Weinsheimer & D. G. Marshall). New York: Continuum (original work published 1975).

Gee, J. P. (2014). *An introduction to discourse analysis: Theory and method.* New York, NY: Routledge.

Gould, S. J. (2002). *The structure of evolutionary theory.* Cambridge, MA: Harvard University Press.

Graham, D. W. (2015). 'Heraclitus.' In E. N. Zalta (Ed.), *The Stanford encyclopedia of philosophy* (Fall 2015 Edition). <http://plato.stanford.edu/archives/fall2015/entries/heraclitus/> accessed August 22, 2015.

Graham, L. J. (2011). The product of text and 'other' statements: Discourse analysis and the critical use of Foucault. *Educational Philosophy and Theory, 43*(6), 663–74.

Greene, M. (1988). *The dialectic of freedom.* New York, NY: Teachers College Press.

Gregory, F. (1977). Scientific versus dialectical materialism: A clash of ideologies in nineteenth-century German radicalism. *Isis, 68*(2), 206–23.

Hacking, I. (1983). *Representing and intervening: Introductory topics in the philosophy of natural science.* Cambridge, UK: Cambridge University Press.

Ho, D. Y. F. (2000). Dialectical thinking: Neither eastern nor western. *American Psychologist, 55*(9), 1064–5.

Hoffmeyer, J. F. (1994). *The advent of freedom: The presence of the future in Hegel's logic.* Cranbury, NJ: Associated University Presses.

Jorgensen, E. R. (2005). Four philosophical models of the relation between theory and practice. *Philosophy of Music Education Review, 13*(1), 21–36.

Kain, P. J. (1980). Marx's dialectic method. *History and Theory: Studies in the Philosophy of History, 19*(3), 294–312.

Kohli, R. (2012). Racial pedagogy of the oppressed: Critical interracial dialogue for teachers of color. *Equity & Excellence in Education, 45*(1), 181–96.

Lather, P. (1986). Research as praxis. *Harvard Educational Review, 56*(3), 257–77.

Lather, P. (1991). *Getting smart: Feminist research and pedagogy with/in the postmodern.* New York, NY: Routledge.

Levinson, M. (1995). Pre- and post-dialectical materialisms: Modeling praxis without subjects and objects. *Cultural Critique, 31,* 111–27.

Luke, A. (1995–1996). Text and discourse in education: An introduction to critical discourse analysis. *Review of Research in Education, 21,* pp. 3–48.

Madison, D. S. (2011). *Critical ethnography: Method, ethics, and performance* (2nd edn.). Thousand Oaks, CA: Sage.

Mitchell, C., DeLange, N., Moletsane, R., Stuart, J., & Buthelezi, T. (2005). Giving a face to HIV and AIDS: On the uses of photo-voice by teachers and community health care workers working with youth in rural South Africa. *Qualitative Research in Psychology, 2*(3), 257–70.

New, C. (1998). Realism, deconstruction and the feminist standpoint. *Journal for the Theory of Social Behaviour, 28*(4), 34–72.

Pascale, C.-M. (2005). There's no place like home: The discursive creation of homelessness. *Cultural Studies <=> Critical Methodologies, 5*(2), 250–68.

Payne, Y. A., & Hamdi, H. A. (2009). "Street love": How street life oriented U. S. born African men frame giving back to one another and the local community. *Urban Review, 41,* 29–46.

Rajchman, J. (1985). *Michel Foucault: The freedom of philosophy.* New York, NY: Columbia University Press.

Rescher, N. (2007). *Dialectics: A classical approach to inquiry.* Frankfurt, Germany: Ontos Verlag.

Roberts, J. M. (2014). Critical realism, dialectics, and qualitative research methods. *Journal for the Theory of Social Behaviour, 44*(1), 1–23. (DOI: 10.1111/jtsb.12056).

Rorty, R. M. (1992). *The linguistic turn: Essays in philosophical method with two retrospective essays.* Chicago, IL: The University of Chicago Press.

Teira, D. (2011). 'Continental philosophies of the social sciences.' In I. C. Jarvie and J. Zamora-Bonilla (Eds.), *The Sage handbook of the philosophy of social sciences* (pp. 81–102). London, UK: Sage.

Todd, S. (2009). Can there be pluralism without conflict? *Philosophy of Education Yearbook,* 51–9.

Van de Ven, A. H., & Poole, M. S. (1995). Explaining development and change in organizations. *Academy of Management Review, 20*(3), 510–40.

Wan, P. Y. (2012). Dialectics, complexity, and the systematic approach: Toward a critical reconciliation. *Philosophy of the Social Sciences, 43*(4), 411–52.

Wetherell, M. (2001). 'Themes in discourse research: The case of Diana.' In M. Wetherell, S. Taylor, & S. J. Yates (Eds.), *Discourse theory and practice: A reader* (pp. 14–28). London, UK: Sage.

Ziersch, A. M., Gallaher, G., Baum, F., & Bentley, M. (2011). Responding to racism: Insights on how racism can damage health from an urban study of Australian Aboriginal people. *Social Science & Medicine, 73,* 1045–53.

5

POETICAL THINKING

Imagine a thinking that could penetrate into certain otherwise hard-to-reach places, like dental floss between the wisdom teeth or an endoscope into the stomach. It will make certain places visible for the very first time—individual branches of the otherwise intractable psychic cave system that runs through the bodies of all humans and can be discovered only by a resourceful imagination audaciously pushing forward into still unsecured galleries. This thinking is poetic thinking, and it is not the exclusive domain of poets and literati; rather, it is a method used by many small search parties that have started out from several directions unbeknownst to one another, an army of phenomenologists working on expanding the confines of our shared imaginaries.

Durs Grünbein, 2010, pp. 90–1

Introduction to Poetical Thinking

As poet Durs Grünbein's quote suggests, poetical thinking is not about art per se, but about unleashing our perceptual, aesthetical capacities for sensual knowing. It is *felt* experience; the experience of *being in* the whirlpool of sensuous flow that we *are* as experiencing beings. This is a move away from an epistemological and representational form of knowing to an ontological one. Poetical thinking is non-representational thinking. It does not concern itself with portraying an experience, understanding, or event as evidence of something else; it is *itself* an experience, an understanding, an event. Philosopher Susanne Langer explains:

The appearances of events in our actual lives are fragmentary, transient and often indefinite, like most of our experiences—like the space we

move in, the time we feel passing, the human and inhuman forces that
challenge us. The poet's business is to create the appearance of "experiences," the semblance of events lived and felt, and to organize them
so they constitute a purely and completely experienced reality, a piece
of *virtual life*.

Langer, 1953, p. 212

The task of the poet then is to capture felt sensations and to turn them back
on to the world for others to experience, as "co-creators" (Avison, 2002, as
quoted in Leggo, 2009, p. 163), as if they too were caught up in this web and
flow of experienced existence. The engagement between poet and audience,
therefore, is an important part of keeping this experiential flow alive. The
minute we (audience or poet/researcher) step out of the experience into an
explanatory or reflective discourse *on* the experience, we have stepped away
from that which is gained from poetical thinking. Poet Zali Gurevitch gives us
some insight into this process:

> To write poetry or poetic writing means to engage in the break of
> language. A beginning not out of nowhere but rather out of end. The
> new question is not how not to finalize or how to disrupt closure but
> rather how to begin. Poetic speech is neither talk (ethnography, narrative,
> theory) nor dance (magic, trance, play) but is between them. So, it is not
> a matter of choosing that side or the other but rather the desire to return
> to dance at the break of dance.
>
> *Gurevitch, 2000, p. 6*

How do we "return to dance at the break of dance"? A good example of this
can be found in Peter Clough's (2002) narrative fictions. He writes that what he
has strived for in his work is "to blur distinctions not only between form and
content, but also between researcher and researched, between data and imagination; to insist, that is, *that language itself, by itself, does the work of inquiry*, without
recourse to the meta-languages of methodology" (pp. 2–3, my emphasis). Unlike
the other three thinking strategies covered so far, what differentiates poetical
thinking is its reach beyond a search for knowledge or meaning into the sensual,
efferent and afferent, difficult-to-grasp, or to put into words, experiential world.
It brings into being the complexities of sensed experiences. Like the wind, it
cannot be seen but its effects are powerful and real. For example, when we
experience a winter wind blowing against our faces or the rush of fright from
an encounter with a snarling dog, we experience simultaneously the cold rise of
the epidermis, the rush of blood in our ears, the rustling of every other moving
object out of sight's reach, and whether I am actually talking about fear or the
wind does not matter, the desire in the poetic is to bring forward the complexity
of sensation, to open up this felt space, and invite you in.

A call for a blurring of art and science is not new, and researchers often find themselves wondering how to resolve what they feel is an unnatural separation imposed by dominant conceptions of research that require a specific scientific method (Eisner, 1981). Like others, whether they perceive themselves to be poets or artist-researchers, or like me do not, the turbulence of life and the complexities of research have propelled many into poetic thinking (see, for example, Beasley, 2007; Brady, 2004; Chawla, 2006; Clough, 1996; Durham, 2004; Flores, 1982; Freeman, 2001b; Furman, 2007; Richardson, 1993; Tedlock, 1999; Wiebe & Snowber, 2011). For example, while the design for my dissertation was simple—interviewing research participants on their experiences with parental involvement—making sense of the complex intersection between theory (what I thought I was doing by drawing on a critical framework) and practice (being there, listening, and seeking understanding) was not. Poetry just happened to be a space where I gave myself over to understanding, not as something outside myself or achievable, but something I was already in the midst of. In poetry, I was able to move from a position as a prepared knower:

> I try to walk you down the corridor
> I had prepared
> And you try to follow me there too
>
> *Freeman, 2001b, p. 646*

to one of recognizing understanding as something lived, experienced, and yet undefined:

> I laugh when I think
> That I feared
> They'd get lost
> When I have never known
> Where I was going
>
> *Freeman, 2001b, p. 657*

Like many researchers, I did not explicitly use poetical strategies in my study of parental involvement, yet neither did I dismiss the aesthetics of the research experience as non-essential components of the meaning-making process. Aesthetics can be understood here as "configurations of experience that create new modes of sense perception" (Rancière, 2004, p. 9). And perception, as psychologist James Hillman explains in his book, *City & Soul*, was rooted in the heart before ever being considered a part of the mind:

> In the ancient world the organ of perception was the heart. The heart was immediately connected to things via the senses. The word for perception or sensation in Greek was *aisthesis*, which means at root a

breathing in or taking in of the world, the gasp, "aha," the "uh" of the breath in wonder, shock, amazement, an aesthetic response to the image (*eidelon*) presented.

Hillman, 2006, p. 36

Perception, therefore, is as much a sensing of, as it is a taking in of, the world. Perception is reception; the ability to actively open oneself up to aesthetic sensing. It is in this way that I conceptualize poetical thinking. It is a way "to impart the sensation of things as they are perceived and not as they are known" (Shklovsky, 1965, p. 12). It requires that we fine-tune "the figurative schemes of thought" (Gibbs, 1994, p. 3) we use in everyday talk, and rethink the role art plays in society and, therefore, in social research. Literary theorist Victor Shklovsky explains:

> The technique of art is to make objects "unfamiliar", to make forms difficult, to increase the difficulty and length of perception because the process of perception is an aesthetic end in itself and must be prolonged. *Art is a way of experiencing the artfulness of an object; the object is not important.*
>
> *Shklovsky, 1965, p. 12*

Rooted in phenomenological conceptions of experience, perception, and language, the approaches of poetical thinking seek to reveal experience as it is experienced, not as it is thought. It requires a deep attentiveness or attunement to the experience of being in the world in all its mundane but complex everydayness. "The phenomenologist's call 'to the things themselves' . . . is an appeal not to literalism but to the generative power that is freed when the human mind listens to what things have to say" (Simms, 2008, p. 1). It blurs a distinction between human and world, and accepts that meaning is created in the experiential space inhabited by both. Ecological philosopher David Abram explains:

> By acknowledging such links between the inner, psychological world and the perceptual terrain that surrounds us, we begin to turn inside-out, loosening the psyche from its confinement within a strictly human sphere, freeing sentience to return to the sensible world that contains us. Intelligence is no longer ours alone but is a property of the earth; we are in it, of it, immersed in its depths.
>
> *Abram, 1996, p. 262*

Characteristics of Poetical Thinking

Poetical thinking is another form of thinking that is not alien to us. We are not only surrounded by human forms of aesthetic expression (for example, music, dance, poetry, art), we often find ourselves taken aback by the sheer beauty of a landscape or the felt depth of an emotion. Although speaking about literature, Shklovsky's quote aptly captures the way art calls on us to prolong the experience of experiencing. It is this dwelling in experience for its own rewards that makes poetical thinking so antithetical to modern-day thinking. So accustomed are we to picturing ourselves as separate beings who act on the world, and whose actions are meant to produce a measurable effect, that the idea that we might be most ourselves in a participatory state of being, where "the invisible shapes of smells, rhythms of cricketsong, and the movement of shadows all, in a sense, provide the subtle body of our thoughts" (Abram, 1996, p. 262), requires a radical reconceptualization of humans in the world. So how should we understand this space of heightened felt senses, this blurring between subject and world that transcends taken-for-granted notions of our centrality and purpose in the world?

Clearly, as has been the case for all the modes of thinking, poetical thinking is a more varied approach than can be presented here. Furthermore, art and poetry also play a significant role in research where narrative or dialectical modes of thinking prevail. Often the presence of an expressive, evocative, and imaginative artistic approach works hand in hand with the narrative presentation of a lived history or the dialectical analysis of an historical event. In many ways, the familiarity of the dialectical encounter, and of the lived experience of the narrative, both contributed to the development and legitimation of poetical thinking as a form of inquiry. Maxine Greene (1986) explains: "Poems address our freedom; they call on us to move beyond where we are, to break with submergence, to transform. To transform what—and how? To move beyond ourselves—and where?" (p. 429). And anthropologist poet Ivan Brady adds:

> Whether posited as reading writing or speaking thinking, sung out in shamanic rhythms, or just whispered in a mirror, . . . poetics is every bit a sensuous-intellectual activity—centering, decoding, reframing, discovering, and discoursing ourselves in ways that show us something of what we are, literally, as embodied participants and observers.
>
> *Brady, 2009, p. xiv*

As embodied perceiver-receivers, poetics—from the Greek verb *poein,* "making," (Hymes, 2000)—calls upon our capacities to engage with "art as a form of *world-making*" (de la Fuente, 2013, p. 169). However, art here should not be conceived of as something separate from the art-maker, nor should it be understood as something under the control of the art-maker. Poet activist Audre Lorde (2009) explains this relationship well: "Poetry is not a luxury. . . . [It is] illumination, for it is through poetry that we give name to those ideas which are, until the poem, nameless and formless, about to be birthed, but already felt" (p. 185). Poetry as illumination requires artists-researchers to blur, and reject, many assumed boundaries and open their senses to all that the world—human and nonhuman—offers. This includes blurring disciplinary boundaries (Brady, 2004; Furman, Szto, & Langer, 2008), recognition of the entanglement of "the verbal and the visual" (Richardson, M., 1994, p. 78), and a shift from "speaking about things . . . [to] language itself as matter, or as that which matters" (Gurevitch, 1999, p. 526). In other words, it requires a reconsideration of one's place in the world, a turning over of oneself to the sensuous; an entangling of subject and object, so that it is not clear whether the artist or the material is leading the creative process (de la Fuente, 2013).

Poetry and art are believed to get us closest to this embodied, immersed state of being. This is where the overlap with narrative is most evident. However, distinct from narrative thinking, the aim of poetical thinking is not to share the experience in its contextualized and temporal form, but to transcend time, space, action, and personal identity, and give oneself over to "the aesthetic state" itself: "a pure instance of suspension, a moment when form is experienced for itself" (Rancière, 2004, p. 44). A poem, or other kind of poetical performance, creates a virtual world *of* meaning, feeling, thought, or event that is thought to be more real than if it was depicting an actual world. Langer (1953) talks about this as "the world of the poem" (p. 228).

This does not mean that poetical thinking is not a deeply personal act. Since poets act as perceiver-receivers, the worlds they create are "full of touch, smell, taste, hearing, and vision, open to the buzz and the joy and the sweat and the tears—the erotics—of daily life" (Brady, 2004, p. 628). In a poem called *Verbal exchange*, Aisha Durham reveals this sense of nakedness:

> I want to be
> A poet, but I am
> Afraid—I can't—stomach putting
> Me out there
> On paper
> For strangers to rummage through my privates
> Like bargain hunters at a Saturday morning yard sale
>
> *Durham, 2004, p. 493*

As the artist-researcher gives him- or herself over to the creative act of art-making, "meaning is made" (Brady, 2004, p. 624), but meaning made in this way is always a transaction, a passing over of one embodied interpretation to the next. Once released, the work of art or the flow of the poem becomes its own thing. So while deeply personal, poetical thinking seeks to transcend the idea of authorship. The speaking "I," Miles Richardson (1994) explains, is no longer relevant as a singular or authorial "I." The artist-researcher together "with the transcending word . . . search to find the luminous instance, that silence that shakes every poet and every ethnographer by opening the way to something close to fear and near to love" (p. 84).

Poetical thinking, therefore, is a fundamental way of experiencing the world. We may not all have the creative ability to write a poem, imagine a sculpture, or perform a play, but we can heighten our awareness and tune our senses to the complex richness of the phenomenal world. As participants in a shared world, poetic thinking is indebted to, but transcends, linguistic and cultural forms of seeing, saying and knowing, juxtaposing, and transposing, forms of saying and perceiving, in ways that move beyond the constraints of any one language (Tedlock, 1999; Tyler, 1984). Speaking about these cross-cultural mixings, Dennis Tedlock (1999) argues: "The poem itself testifies to the existence of alternative ways of saying something and implies that there could still be others" (p. 157). In general, therefore, poetical thinking:

1. *Privileges the figurative and performative dimensions of languages, images, and gestures over their literal or representational ones.* Poetical thinking requires that we let languages, bodies, movements, or images lead the way (Barthes, 1982). As linguistic and symbolic beings, we all have the capacity to participate in the becoming of language, that is, to imagine, to be, to feel, and to mean something different through these imaginings. In this way of thinking, art practices are a form of human participation in meaning-making that gives "form to thought" (Sullivan, 2006, p. 29). However, the form that is generated from the encounter always surpasses the intent of those involved, including the artist. This is because an aesthetic object or experience always "exceed[s] all interpretation" (Davey, 2013, p. 3), and serves as a catalyst for new meanings or the not yet thought (Heidegger, 1968). Art educator Elliot Eisner explains the potential of this kind of thinking for social science research:

> What art seeks is not the discovery of . . . laws . . . but rather the creation of images that people will find meaningful and from which their fallible and tentative views of the world can be altered, rejected, or made more secure.
>
> *Eisner, 1981, p. 9*

This requires a conceptual shift about the aims of research. Rather than view social science research primarily as a way to examine and represent people's meanings or their social worlds, poetical thinking asks that we acknowledge the power and presence of figurative thinking at the center of thought. Psycholinguist Raymond Gibbs explains its function:

> Metaphor, metonymy, irony, and other tropes are not linguistic distortions of literal mental thought but constitute basic schemes by which people conceptualize their experience and the external world. Since every mental construct reflects an adaptation of the mind to the world, the

language that expresses these constructs attests to the continuous process of poetic thinking.

Gibbs, 1994, p. 1

The aim, therefore, of poetic forms of inquiry is not *an* interpretation of the perceptual encounter but an invitation for others to enter the phenomenal world of human experience. In other words, the truth or meaning of an artistic or poetical performance does not precede its reception, nor does the receiver need to agree with the artist's view, or any other receiver's view for that matter.

2. *Mediates between real and possible felt worlds in ways that open up rather than close the potential for multiple interpretations.* Poetical thinking merges world and experience in pursuit of aesthetic ways to recirculate worldly meanings onto themselves. Artists and poetical researchers enter a world already in motion and seek ways to move with it. Philosopher Richard Kearney (1998) explains: "The being of the human subject, as a being who innovates, is not a fixed point but an endless spiral of movement. The origin of poetic imagining is neither a transcendental ego nor a negating *pour soi*—it is a becoming of language which demands perpetual rebirth" (p. 111). Together, with every word and every image, poetical thinkers open the world up to what philosopher James Risser (2002) calls an "infinite dialogue." And it is dialogue that characterizes the movement of poetical thinking, rather than dialectics. Although, as discussed in Chapter 4, dialogue can be dialectical, the dialogue of poetical thinking works from within the middle of dialectics, the generative space of multiplicity. Rather than seek synthesis and transformation into something else (as dialectical thinking often aims to do), the dialogical movement of poetical thinking makes full use of the ontological, generative space of becoming (Gadamer, 1989). Furthermore, poetical thinking is inherently a practical activity (Gadamer, 1981). The world in all of its concreteness, whether directly experienced, or experienced through language, images, and gestures, is a dialogical partner (Davey, 2013; Gadamer, 1989). This relationship is kinetic as media scholar Julian Henriques (2010) argues: "We not only feel moved *by* something, but are also moved to *do* something—to take action and move others" (p. 73). The world beckons us and we respond (Heidegger, 1968), not by taking it over or shaping it to our image, but by participating in its unfolding; a participation that requires letting go and taking risks. "We do not enter into dialogue, we find ourselves already in it—but only if we are already listening with the most intense attention, all ears to the discreet, the whispered word. Dialogue has no guarantees, being pure risk" (Marshall, 2004, p. 143).

This generative space of becoming is, however, paradoxical. Like poetry, it "is never as unified as when it diversifies" (Bachelard, 1969, p. 25). This is because art and poetry maximize the expressive quality of the work of art by keeping the possibilities of its "meaning" in flux, and, yet, each work of art is uniquely itself (Davey, 2013; Gadamer, 1989). Gadamer explains: "Becoming

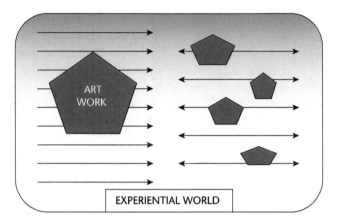

FIGURE 5.1   Poetics as Infinite Dialogue

is no longer simply some kind of nonbeing, that is, something seen as the becoming of something different: . . . it signifies coming into being. . . . Being emerges from becoming!" (2007, p. 209, as quoted in Davey, 2013, p. 126). What makes a work of art or novel worth seeing or reading again is that its meaning is not readily available to us, and each new reading, each viewing, will provoke us in new ways, provide us with new possible considerations of what it might be. And while the work forms a unity, it is not self-enclosed; its meaning exceeds itself in ways that even the artist could not imagine. Figure 5.1 illustrates this unending movement.

So, although poetical thinking blurs boundaries, this does not mean that one thing gets subsumed in the other. On the contrary, what is constructed belongs to the dialogical event itself, whether conceived of as understanding (Gadamer, 1989), aesthetic experience (Rancière, 2004), or some other construct. As participants in the event, poetical thinkers too are transformed, however this transformation does not stand apart from the event that produced it. Poetical thinking, therefore, mediates the "polyphony of the senses" (Bachelard, 1969, p. 6), and puts into motion complex, difficult-to-articulate, human felt experiences. There is no original experience represented. Rather, the "original" experience is kept alive, developed, becoming more than originally imagined or intended. This notion of repetition takes a posthuman form in diagrammatical thinking discussed in Chapter 6, but here it is deeply human, its aim is to engage, bring out that which is human about humanity, or the potential of humanity in humans. It helps re-create experiences that may otherwise be lost or create those that have not yet been thought.

3. Invites, even requires, participation, dwelling, a desire to be transformed, an activist engagement with "the polyphony of the senses" rather than a passive one. Poetical thinking requires participation, a perceiver-receiver, a sharing of the experience for it to make a difference in the world. Understanding, perceiving, and feeling take shape within an active involvement and "a long lingering with the senses" (Wiebe & Snowber, 2011, p. 106). And while this dwelling entails a deep listening to the "other," this should not be understood as a neutral event. Poetical thinking is inherently political, although perhaps not in the usual practice of the word as some form of taking sides on an issue. Rather, its aim is to intervene "in the general distribution of ways of doing and making" (Rancière, 2004, p. 13).

In his book, *Narratives and fictions in educational research,* Clough (2002) explains that the problem with research validity is that it depends "on things being already what/as they are" (p. 93). What he means is that scientific notions of validity set up a solipsistic situation where to know requires an already defined conception of what can be known and what knowledge looks like. Art, however, disrupts this assumption by revealing itself as having its *"own intentionalistic structure"* (Clough, 2002, p. 94), where meaning is accomplished in every encounter, encounters that do not need to "make sense" (Furman, 2007) in any traditional sense of the word. Taking an aesthetic approach, according to philosopher Jacques Rancière, initiates a different

> kind of relation between sense and sense, a supplement that both reveals and neutralizes the division at the heart of the sensible. Let us call it a *dissensus.* A dissensus is not a conflict; it is a perturbation of the normal relation between sense and sense.
>
> *Rancière, 2009, p. 3*

One way of understanding this perturbation is to understand the work of art as a performance; an event that is neither separate from the work or "represents" the work in any preconceived way (Gadamer, 1989). Philosopher Nicholas Davey explains this relationship:

> The world is not art and yet the world requires art in order for us to discern what worldly action is possible. . . . It is not a question of translating the image into actuality but of allowing that image to transform one's understanding of what is plausible or possible within actuality.
>
> *Davey, 2013, p. 134*

In other words, poetical thinking seeks to engage while also shocking us out of our complacency, keeping images and words from ever becoming fixed (Gurevitch, 2000). It "demands of us that we engage ourselves with what at first sight does not go together at all" (Heidegger, 1966, p. 53). Although he is discussing Martin Heidegger's style of writing, Robert Mugerauer's description captures well this kind of encounter with a work of art:

> Before Heidegger can motivate us to try to understand, he must make us take notice. We notice that we read and think, but do we understand

what that is? Do we examine the ground of our reading and thinking, our facile use of words? To bend us toward such notice, he throws things in that disturb our train of thought. Most likely he disturbs us, *not from thought, but into it.*

Mugerauer, *1988, p. 7 (my emphasis added)*

Because dialogue presumes the presence of an other, whether the other is a work of art, another person, or the world itself, to be disturbed into thought demands a suspension (Rancière, 2004) of preconceived attitudes or judgment of seeing the "other" as separate from ourselves. The "other" is a co-creator of meaning; a meaning that does not belong to either one of us. It is only in this way that a breaking down of the dichotomous thinking of dialectics can be achieved.

4. *When successful, poetical thinking transcends its human origins, becoming more "world" than "human," more felt collectivity than individuality.* Poetical thinking puts humans into the midst of living; a living that precedes and extends beyond any mortal existence. Because language and meaning belong to the world (Halliburton, 1981), and not to any one being, poetry and art serve as a medium with which to enter this flow. It is, by its very nature, a movement that is larger than all of us put together. As such, thinking poetically puts us in the midst of movement. It does not claim to understand, to complete a thought, or to still the movement of becoming. As participants in the world, humans have the potential to contribute in meaningful ways to the unfolding of meaning and understanding. Meaning and understanding, by their very nature, however, are movements that will always exceed any possibility of totality, so there are no guarantees that one's engagement will be beneficial or harmful, only that there is the potential to effect the flow of humanity or the "topography of the thinkable" (Rancière, 2009, p. 19).

It is this potentiality—this infinite excess—that serves as an invitation, rather than as a deterrent. Poet researcher Carl Leggo (2009) explains: "Poets call to one another, a chorus of voices, calling out, calling together, seeking readers and writers to join in the co-creation of texts that are alive in the world" (p. 163). Being alive in the midst of meaning keeps felt experience alive and moving through generations of perceiver-receivers, each encounter putting into motion multiple and enduring effects and new articulations of meaning. Poetical researchers engage in this movement, not because they believe that there is an essential or original meaning to be found, but because they understand that all meaning is dynamic and has potential to be enhanced, redirected, thwarted, changed, or even obliterated. Poets participate in this flow because it is only by participating that growth for all occurs (Lorde, 2009).

Poetical Thinking in Practice

Poetical thinking takes researchers outside a scientific conception of the world to embrace all aspects of the arts, allowing and supporting a variety of expressive forms and purposes. Since its possibilities are only constrained by the limits we impose on our imagination, like the other sections on modes of thinking in practice within this book, the strategies described here only illustrate some of the work artist-researchers are conducting. However, each example shown responds in some way to the questions Ely et al. (1997) posed when thinking about the range of poetical approaches available to them: "How do we animate that which we studied? How do we bring to life what was buried beneath the obvious and literal?" (p. 19).

In general, researchers using poetical thinking strategies believe that providing provocative, artistic expressions of their encounters with their topic of inquiry or data provides a significant contribution to human research. It does this by creating a collaborative, performative space where researchers, participants, and audiences can make sense of lived life together. The sense that is made is not predetermined nor is it meant to be the same for everyone. Some will receive therapeutic benefits from their encounter, while others will be moved to social action. Others will find that dwelling in the complex layers of felt existence unleashes new understandings, new visions, hopes and possibilities. Artist-researchers Sean Wiebe and Celeste Snowber express this experience well:

> The stew of our lives is the ability to live, breathe, and listen to the sensuous world within us and around us. . . . [T]hus to honor how we were created as humans is to find a myriad of ways to bring the senses to learning.
>
> *Wiebe & Celeste, 2011, p. 108*

Earlier I quoted Clough's (2002) statement that in his research "language itself, by itself does the work of inquiry" (p. 3). Add the potentials of linguistic and nonlinguistic forms of expression such as photography, collage, dance, installation, performance, poetry, or fiction and you have a sense of what poetical thinking is capable of doing. Clough's fictional dramas illustrate this kind of work well.

In the following research story, Clough is a home-school relations officer at a school for children with special educational needs. In the excerpt below, he had just knocked on the door of a pupil's home—a pupil who was having difficulties which required discussion with a parent. This short excerpt not only presents the situation well but also gives you an idea of Clough's style:

> I had written—twice—that I was coming, but there was no sign of life when I arrived at 11. The curtains were drawn at all the windows and this was the only bungalow where there was no smoke from the chimney though this was a February morning. I knocked and banged and I would have gone just as the door opened.
> —now then, what's the f★★★
> —It's me, Mr . . . It's Mr Clough . . . Mr Clough from the school.

He was trying hard to focus on me; something stirred in him, but he was very drunk—still—and he had woken up too quickly. He was rubbing fiercely at his eyes, kneading the lids down so they creaked and they flashed red meat; and his blue chin rasped as his palms followed the work of his fingers. He was wearing a vest and brown trousers which he had spoiled somehow; there was a wet circle around his groin and then wet across one hip and down to the knee.

I can see myself standing there in my blue Harris tweed jacket and saying '*It's Mr Clough . . . Mr Clough from the school.*' Try it: there are not many ways to say those words and even fewer meanings.

He smelled of spent drink and the smell of the dark house reached out from behind him. Behind him I could see Klaus [the pupil in question] asleep on his back on a settee, open-mouthed and open-limbed.

—Shall I give you time to get up, you're obviously . . . (*obviously* for god's sake) . . . I could come back in . . . an hour?

Clough, 1996, pp. 75–6

As a reader, as painful as it turns out to be, you can't help but be drawn into the story, connecting to each character at an emotional level you may not have been aware that you had. Clough's stories are painful, not because of the mixture of emotions you and the characters go through but because the humanity exhibited, and lack thereof, is *our* humanity, in its rawness, accomplishments, and failings, and you can't help but wonder how it is we constructed such a world for ourselves. Affronting our senses is what Clough seeks. As he explains:

The stories require investment—of energy and emotion and intellect— and so will speak differently to different people. But a common feature of the stories is that they all revolve around difficulty and sometimes tragedy. They are about suffering, misfortune and injustice and have a capacity to shock, to affront.

Clough, 2002, p. 18

Although it is clear that Clough is simultaneously drawing on narrative thinking in the work that he does, his work illustrates poetical thinking because of its non-representational, experiential, and aesthetic qualities. In other words, his fictions are not about a particular setting or individual, although much of what he writes, for example, the encounter with the father shared earlier (Clough, 1996, pp. 75–6), actually happened. By drawing on the aesthetics and multivocality of language itself, his stories present a moral stance and a sense of urgency about very human issues whose verification occur "only in collision with the experience of the reader" (Clough, 2002, p. 62). This is an ongoing encounter. The researcher engages with an issue, a theme of importance, or an encounter with a participant, and then crafts an event for us as readers, to further expand the expressions of the truths which make up our existence. Clough (1996) explains in reference to another story: "When I came to write of Nick there was no method within the means of research [that] would allow me to evoke him for a reader without violating, through reduction, the nervous complex of meanings which meeting and working with him provoked" (p. 73). Research using poetical modes of thinking seeks instead to release that *nervous complex of meanings* so as to engage readers into their own nervous complex of meaning in a continuous movement of being and becoming.

Using different genres of writing is not the only artistic form of expression used by artist-researchers. Painting, dance, theatre, music, or a creative mixture of artistic forms, can now be found, especially at conferences, which lend themselves to alternative forms of performance. For example, Rich Furman, Peter Szto, and Carol Langer (2008) used poetry and photography in their examination of resident life in a psychiatric hospital in China. They created a collaborative process beginning with Peter Szto first developing relationships with mental health patients in a Chinese psychiatric hospital in order to take pictures of their lived experience in the institution. In this first encounter with the topic, the photographs represented "unique social events between photographer and subject" (p. 27). The photographs were then sent to Rich Furman who wrote short poems in response to his encounter with the image. Furman, Szto, and Langer discuss the issues involved with their process which included writing poems in response to the photographs and not based upon the poet's actual visit to the psychiatric hospital, resulting in further removal from the actual event. This, however, was not considered a weakness but became an important part of the meaning event. As they explained: "The poetry therefore serves both as interpretations and as data when presented along with the photographs. Together, they present an evocative expression that can stimulate reflection in the viewer" (p. 35). Opening up artistic productions to an audience does not mean that ethical issues of representation are either resolved or lessened. Rather, the ethical issues, such as, in this example, being a white American male poet writing about the experiences of Chinese psychiatric patients, or representing the experiences of an institutional life one has never experienced, are revealed and become part of the interpretive reading as well.

Even when the performance involves biographical material, as in the work of artist-researcher James Rolling (2008) who writes about the complexities of postmodern identity and the politics of renaming, understanding does not precede the act of writing/producing. On the contrary, "writing without certainty, blasphemous of all borders and predetermination" (p. 942) opens up possibilities for re-inscribing self and practice in ways that might not otherwise be possible. The event of writing, speaking, performing, dancing provokes encounters between the unknown and what was assumed to be known, disrupting deterministic powers of representation and societal expectations. Only then can new forms of understanding take shape, at least temporarily, until they too are dissolved or re-authored in new ways. Rolling (2008) explains: "To unname is to undermine purported origins, to burrow between the archaeologies that constrain, to initiate and inaugurate anomalous genealogies that thrive and proliferate and die and leach new life between layers" (p. 934).

Art allows artists to transform their lived experiences "into transcended configurations" (van Manen, 1990, p. 74) whose reach extends into the unknown. Furthermore, embedded in the arts is a deeply aesthetic way of knowing that enables artist-researchers to confront the limitations of traditional research standards and seek new ways of engaging with life and living. In this process, the art itself, whether words, images, or movements, gains its own agency and invites repeated engagements into its being and becoming.

Deciding on Poetical Thinking for Analysis

There are many ways that artistic practices have been used in research design. However, not all arts-based research prioritizes or makes use of poetical thinking in the way described here. For example, poetic transcription, poems constructed from and grounded in the data "move in the direction of poetry but [are] not necessarily poetry" (Glesne, 1997, p. 213). Similarly, an artistic approach might be taken up in unique and compelling ways but, in many cases, the principles guiding the work are more likely aligned with a narrative or dialectical standpoint. This does not make the work less significant, only that it is important to recognize what distinguishes these if gaining a deeper understanding of poetical thinking is desired. What clearly differentiates poetical thinking from the others is that the aesthetic experience that is opened up in the encounter between an artist and the world, or an audience and a work of art (such as the poetry, installation, performance of an artist-researcher), puts into motion the varied possibilities of a world of potential; a "moment of transcendence" (Davey, 2013, p. 133) that gives us a glimpse of humanity's truth without corresponding to any actual truth. It is this unrealized (and never-ending) potential that artist-researchers build on and develop further in their work. Therefore, using poetical thinking strategies in research requires entering into an aesthetic, experiential relationship with your research topic rather than one guided by the conventions of social science research (Freeman, 2011; Schwandt, 2004).

In general, poetical thinking allows researchers to:

• Penetrate the felt and difficult-to-grasp regions of experiential life
• Reach beyond meaning and keep understanding in flow
• Create expressions of encounters that expand and challenge the imagination
• Critique what is, by creating what is not yet thought possible

Like the other modes of thinking presented in this text, poetical thinking is constrained by its inherent structure, and is not without its challenges or criticisms. In regards to decision-making, the primary ones addressed here are negotiating competing standards of quality and art as research.

Competing standards of quality. One challenge to conducting research guided by poetical thinking strategies is that it will be assessed for its artistic qualities as well as for its contribution to what advances it makes about the topic of inquiry. So even if you do not consider yourself to be an artist, some ability or training in the arts is an important criterion for this kind of work. Artist-researchers Kent Maynard and Melisa Cahnmann-Taylor explain:

> Ethnographic poetry should not be judged by more forgiving criteria than poetry at large. The purposes of truth-telling ethnography are not served by writing inferior verse. Whether it is good or bad, poetry remains a cultural convention, just as ethnographic writing is.
>
> *Maynard & Cahnmann-Taylor, 2010, p. 12*

This means that artist-researchers must be able to work across often competing standards of quality, which involves understanding the conventions of both, even while seeking to transcend these in order to integrate often disparate forms of thinking and expression (Bresler, 2006). Although there are disagreements about what these are, most people have certain expectations in regards to assessing the quality of research and art, and these are not diminished as a result of their mixing. Art educator Liora Bresler (2006) argues: "Good qualitative research, like art, presents us with complex reality. Bad research and art, I suggest, distort in the process of oversimplification, creating stereotypes and distancing us from the world" (p. 65). And educator Tom Barone (2002), in a commentary on the blurring of art and science, adds support to this perspective:

> The design elements that are common to arts-based research projects are, I suggest, like those found in any good research, not present for their own sake. Nor are they chosen at random. Their selection is evidence of recognition that in successful research endeavors form and function are mutually supportive.
>
> *Barone, 2002, p. 258*

In general, arts-based researchers agree that this kind of research requires a deep sense of design and appreciation of aesthetics. Eisner (2002) states: "Artistry requires sensibility, imagination, technique, and the ability to make judgments about the feel and significance of the particular" (p. 382). Furthermore, art is valued for its ability to promote critical action so arts-based research is inherently political. Denzin asserts:

> These texts are sites of resistance. They are places where meanings, politics, and identities are negotiated. They transform and challenge all

forms of cultural representation . . . [and] should be valued for the collective and individual reflection and critical action [they produce] . . . including conversations that cross the boundaries of race, class, gender, and nation.

Denzin, 2000, pp. 259–60

In other words, poetical thinkers seek "transgressive validity" (Richardson, 1993). Sociologist Laurel Richardson (1993) explains what this might look like: "By settling words together in new configurations, the relations created through echo, repetition, rhythm, rhyme let us hear and see the world in a new dimension. Poetry is thus a *practical* and *powerful* means for reconstitution of worlds" (p. 705). In this way, validity is reached when the encounter achieves a "living presence, a presence that involves researchers in a dynamic, intimate dialogue that the research's audience can consequently also experience" (Bresler, 2006, p. 61), and pushes that audience "to think in ways that may be revolutionary" (Dillard, 2014, p. 255). This reception need not be the same for everyone, and in fact, should not be. The variety of ways that poetry, or other forms of artistic performance, have been received in the social sciences are also an indication of its ability to recreate itself in new ways. For example, after sharing a poem founded on the interview transcripts of a woman whom Richardson (1993) named "Louisa May," she took note of its reception by different academic groups. Although some groups "challenged the 'validity' of the poem" (p. 133), Richardson explained that many saw this as an opportunity to deepen new methodological and representational paths emerging among feminist and poststructural researchers. The point here is that this diversity of effects, even conflicting ones, is considered positive for poetical thinkers who see validity as emanating from having a continued effect on the world. The decision to approach research from this perspective would support research projects that seek to provoke an aesthetic response in others or, as mentioned earlier, to disturb others "into thought."

Art as research. Research shaped by the arts or poetical thinking is usually well-received and appreciated for its ability to provoke an aesthetic response and resist the dominant scientific paradigm. Less certain, however, is how to assess its status as research, and whether such a status is even necessary. Artist-researchers disagree on this issue. Some believe that, although an arts-based researcher might have a different criterion for the quality and aim of a study, seeking legitimacy within the larger research community is an important goal, and that one way of doing this is "by explicating the logic-of-justification that underpins his or her work" (Piantanida, McMahon, & Garman, 2003, p. 185). Others feel that attaining legitimacy as research undermines the important transgressive role played by the arts and that "arts-based researchers must undergo a radical break from science as a standpoint for understanding" (Finley, 2003, p. 289). Still others believe that the false separation between art and science is the issue. Art, research, and science are all in the business of creating meaning and knowledge about the world. By aligning itself with a narrow view of science, research has disregarded the essential aesthetic qualities of science (Eisner, 2006) and created its own problematic dichotomy. For Eisner, arts-based research "is an expression of the need for diversity and a tendency to push towards a de-standardization of method" (2006, p. 16). In other words, the proliferation of various forms of arts-based research is evidence that science needs art, not that art needs science. Finally, related to these concerns is that research and art both need audiences if they are to have any effect. Since the primary mode for disseminating research results is text-based, finding appropriate venues for sharing one's work can be challenging. Fortunately, this too is changing. Many conferences already provide spaces for performances, dances, installations, and so forth. And several journals are taking advantage of the access to multimedia offered by the Internet (see, for example, *Liminalities: A Journal of Performance Studies*).

Poetic thinking transcends borders, connecting, as well as dissolving and rearranging, a dynamic world of felt experiences. It takes the central movement of living to heart, keeping that movement alive while also participating in its recreation and dispersion. Poetical thinking has contributed to the ontological turn in the social sciences (Gadamer, 1989). It has done so from a deep-seated belief in the centrality of humans as co-creators of the world's meaning structures. So although poetical thinkers believe the world—in the sense that things, whether natural or humanly-made—have equal "voice," the ontological space resides within these human structures of meaning. As shown in Chapter 6, a general critique of this focus on human meaning has been one of the catalysts for the development of diagrammatical strategies in the social sciences. By moving from human-world co-creations as forms of aesthetic relationships to assemblages of things as manifestations of movement itself, meaning is displaced. In this final displacement of the human, things—humans or otherwise—gain power and presence by virtue of the intensity emanating from assemblages. This move takes us beyond "the mode of the thing itself" and into a radical rethinking of ontology.

References

Abram, D. (1996). *The spell of the sensuous: Perception and language in a more-than-human world*. New York, NY: Pantheon Books.

Bachelard, G. (1969). *The poetics of reverie* (trans. from French by Daniel Russell). New York, NY: The Orion Press.

Barone, T. (2002). From genre blurring to audience blending: Reflections on the field emanating from an ethnodrama. *Anthropology & Education Quarterly, 33*(2), 255–67.

Barthes, R. (1982). *A Barthes reader* (Edited, and with an introduction, by Susan Sontag). New York, NY: Hill and Wang.

Beasley, L. (2007). Vestigial. *Anthropology and Humanism, 32*(2), 210.

Brady, I. (2004). In defense of the sensual: Meaning construction in ethnography and poetics. *Qualitative Inquiry, 10*(4), 622–44.

Brady, I. (2009). 'Foreword.' In M. Prendergast, C. Leggo, & P. Sameshima (Eds.), *Poetic inquiry: Vibrant voices in the social sciences* (pp. xi–xvi). Rotterdam, The Netherlands: Sense Publisher.

Bresler, L. (2006). Toward connectedness: Aesthetically based research. *Studies in Art Education: A Journal of Issues and Research, 48*(1), 52–69.

Chawla, D. (2006). The bangle seller of meena bazaar. *Qualitative Inquiry, 12*(6), 1135–8.

Clough, P. (1996). 'Again fathers and sons': The mutual construction of self, story and special education needs. *Disability & Society, 11*(1), 71–82.

Clough, P. (2002). *Narratives and fictions in educational research.* Buckingham, UK: Open University Press.

Davey, N. (2013). *Unfinished worlds: Hermeneutics, aesthetics and Gadamer.* Edinburgh, UK: Edinburgh University Press.

de la Fuente, E. (2013). Why aesthetic patterns matter: Art and a "qualitative" social theory. *Journal for the Theory of Social Behaviour, 44*(2), 168–85.

Denzin, N. K. (2000). Aesthetics and the practices of qualitative inquiry. *Qualitative Inquiry, 6*(2), 256–65.

Dillard, C. B. (2014). '(Re)membering the grandmothers: Theorizing poetry to (re)think the purposes of black education and research.' In N. K. Denzin & M. D. Giardina (Eds.), *Qualitative inquiry outside the academy* (pp. 253–67). Walnut Creek, CA: Left Coast Press.

Durham, A. (2004). Verbal exchange. *Qualitative Inquiry, 10*(4), 493–4.

Eisner, E. W. (1981). On the differences between scientific and artistic approaches to qualitative research. *Educational Researcher, 10*(4), 5–9.

Eisner, E. W. (2002). From episteme to phronesis to artistry in the study and improvement of teaching. *Teaching and Teacher Education, 18*(4), 375–85.

Eisner, E. (2006). Does arts-based research have a future? *Studies in Art Education: A Journal of Issues and Research, 48*(1), 9–18.

Ely, M., Vinz, R., Downing, M., & Anzul, M. (1997). *On writing qualitative research: Living by words.* Bristol, PA: The Falmer Press.

Finley, S. (2003). Arts-based inquiry in QI: Seven years from crisis to guerrilla warfare. *Qualitative Inquiry, 9*(2), 281–96.

Flores, T. (1982). Field poetry. *Anthropology and Humanism Quarterly, 7*(1), 16–22.

Freeman, M. (2001b). "Between eye and eye stretches an interminable landscape": The challenge of philosophical hermeneutics. *Qualitative Inquiry, 7*(5), 646–58.

Freeman, M. (2011, July). Validity in dialogic encounters with hermeneutic truths. *Qualitative Inquiry, 17*(6), 543–51.

Furman, R. (2007). Poetry and narrative as qualitative data: Explorations into existential theory. *Indo-Pacific Journal of Phenomenology, 7*(1), 1–9.

Furman, R., Szto, P., & Langer, C. (2008). Using poetry and photography as qualitative data: A study of a psychiatric hospital in China. *Journal of Poetry Therapy, 21*(1), 23–37.

Gadamer, H.-G. (1981). *Reason in the age of science* (trans. by Frederick G. Lawrence). Cambridge, MA: The MIT Press.

Gadamer, H.-G. (1989). *Truth and method* (2nd revised edn., trans. by J. Weinsheimer & D. G. Marshall). New York: Continuum (original work published 1975).

Gibbs, R. W. (1994). *The poetics of mind: Figurative thought, language, and understanding.* New York, NY: Cambridge University Press.

Glesne, C. (1997). That rare feeling: Re-presenting research through poetic transcription. *Qualitative Inquiry, 3*(2), 202–21.

Greene, M. (1986). In search of a critical pedagogy. *Harvard Educational Review, 56*(4), 427–41.

Grünbein, D. (2010). *The bars of Atlantis: Selected essays* (trans. by John Crutchfield, Michael Hofmann, and Andrew Shields). New York, NY: Farrar, Straus and Giroux.

Gurevitch, Z. (1999). The tongue's break dance: Theory, poetry, and the critical body. *The Sociological Quarterly, 40*(3) 525–40.

Gurevitch, Z. (2000). The serious play of writing. *Qualitative Inquiry, 6*(1), 3–8.

Halliburton, D. (1981). *Poetic thinking: An approach to Heidegger.* Chicago, IL: The University of Chicago Press.

Heidegger, M. (1966). *Discourse on thinking* (trans. by John M. Anderson and E. Hans Freund). New York, NY: Harper & Row.

Heidegger, M. (1968). *What is called thinking?* (trans. by J. Glenn Gray). New York, NY: Harper & Row.

Henriques, J. (2010). The vibrations of affect and their propagation on a night out on Kingston's dancehall scene. *Body & Society, 16*(1), 57–89.

Hillman, J. (2006). *City & Soul.* Putnam, CN: Spring Publications.

Hymes, D. (2000). Poetry. *Journal of Linguistic Anthropology, 9*(1–2), 191–3.

Kearney, R. (1998). *Poetics of imagining: Modern to post-modern.* Bronx, NY: Fordham University Press.

Langer, S. K. (1953). *Feeling and form: A theory of art.* New York, NY: Charles Scribner's Sons.

Leggo, C. (2009). 'Living love stories: Fissures, fragments, fringes.' In M. Prendergast, C. Leggo, & P. Sameshima (Eds.), *Poetic inquiry: Vibrant voices in the social sciences* (pp. 147–68). Rotterdam, The Netherlands: Sense Publishers.

Lorde, A. (2009). *I am your sister: Collected and unpublished writings of Audre Lorde.* New York, NY: Oxford University Press.

Marshall, D. G. (2004). 'On dialogue: To its cultured despisers.' In B. Krajewski (Ed.), *Gadamer's repercussions: reconsidering philosophical hermeneutics* (pp. 123–44). Berkeley, CA: University of California Press.

Maynard, K., & Cahnmann-Taylor, M. (2010). Anthropology at the edge of words: Where poetry and ethnography meet. *Anthropology and Humanism, 35*(1), 2–19.

Mugerauer, R. (1988). *Heidegger's language and thinking.* Atlantic Highlands, NJ: Humanities Press International.

Piantanida, M., McMahon, P. L., & Garman, N. B. (2003). Sculpting the contours of arts-based educational research within a discourse community. *Qualitative Inquiry, 9*(2), 182–91.

Rancière, J. (2004). *The politics of aesthetics: The distribution of the sensible* (trans. and with introduction by Gabriel Rockhill). New York, NY: Continuum.

Rancière, J. (2009). The aesthetic dimension: Aesthetics, politics, knowledge. *Critical Inquiry, 36,* 1–19.

Richardson, L. (1993). Poetics, dramatics, and transgressive validity: The case of the skipped line. *The Sociological Quarterly, 34*(4), 695–710.

Richardson, M. (1994). Writing poetry and doing ethnography: Aesthetics and observation on the page and in the field. *Anthropology and Humanism, 19*(1), 77–87.

Risser, J. (2002). In the shadow of Hegel: Infinite dialogue in Gadamer's hermeneutics. *Research in Phenomenology, 32,* 86–102.

Rolling, J. H. (2008). Secular blasphemy: Utter(ed) transgressions against names and fathers in the postmodern era. *Qualitative Inquiry, 14*(6), 926–48.

Schwandt, T. A. (2004). 'Hermeneutics: A poetics of inquiry versus a methodology for research.' In H. Piper and I. Stronach (Eds.), *Educational research: Difference and diversity* (pp. 31–44). Burlington, VT: Ashgate.

Shklovsky, V. (1965). 'Art as technique.' In *Russian Formalist Criticism: Four essays* (trans. and with introduction by Lee T. Lemon & Marion J. Reis) (pp. 3–57). Lincoln, NE: University of Nebraska Press.

Simms, E. M. (2008). *The child in the world: Embodiment, time, and language in early childhood.* Detroit, MI: Wayne State University Press.

Sullivan, G. (2006). Research acts in art practice. *Studies in Art Education, 48*(1), 19–35.

Tedlock, D. (1999). Poetry and ethnography: A dialogical approach. *Anthropology and Humanism, 24*(2), 155–67.

Tyler, S. A. (1984). The poetic turn in postmodern anthropology: The poetry of Paul Friedrich. *American Anthropologist, 86*(2), 328–36.

van Manen, M. (1990). *Researching lived experience: Human science for an active sensitive pedagogy.* Albany, NY: State University of New York Press.

Wiebe, S., & Snowber, C. (2011). The visceral imagination: A fertile space for non-textual knowing. *Journal of Curriculum Theorizing, 27*(2), 101–13.

6

DIAGRAMMATICAL THINKING

What matters to me is precisely a displacement of the analytic problematic, making it drift from systems of *statements* and performed subjective *structures* towards *Assemblages of enunciation* able to forge new co-ordinates for reading and to 'bring into existence' new representations and propositions.

Félix Guattari, 2013, p. 17

An abstract machine is characterized by its matter—its hecceities, or relations of speeds and affects—but also by its function. . . . This function is neither semiotic nor physical, neither expression nor content, but an abstract function that informs both the expression-form . . . and the content-form. . . . Such an abstract function, characteristic of every abstract machine, Deleuze and Guattari call a 'diagram'.

Ronald Bogue, 1989, p. 135

Introduction to Diagrammatical Thinking

As these quotes suggest, diagrammatical thinking is not another form of repre-sentational thought[1] but is a form of reading, a *transversal* reading that brings "together without uniting or reducing to one . . . non-communicating frag-ments" (Genosko, 2001, p. 9). It produces a particular kind of assembling of disparate entities that *generates* thought (Watson, 2009). The focus of this reading is not on what an assemblage of parts *mean* but on the question of articulation itself. Furthermore, an assemblage should not be thought of as a representational tool, such as in the diagrammatic representation of a family's genealogy or an organization's administrative structure (although these could be part of the kind of assemblage described in this chapter). Rather, the kind of assemblage discussed here is a moving entity whose articulations produce effects, leaving traces of its passage in the form of rigid and fluid structures and relationships, beneficial and harmful subjectivities, physical and ephemeral manifestations, and is often conceptualized as an assembling that dissolves traditional boundaries between the natural and the social, agency and structure, things and people, experiences and concepts, and so on (Bijker & Law, 1992; Coole & Frost, 2010; Deleuze & Guattari, 1987; Latour, 2005).

A transversal reading works from the middle of an assemblage of disparate entities. Unlike categorical or dialectical thinking, it does not seek identification of the assembled parts or a synthesis of these parts into another. What is at stake is how this middle, the between of things, is itself something else, a state of difference, unnamed and unnameable, but leaving powerful traces as it moves in and out of relationships, changing configurations along the way. Philosophers Gilles Deleuze and Félix Guattari explain:

> The middle is by no means an average; on the contrary, it is where things pick up speed. *Between* things does not designate a localizable relation going from one thing to the other and back again, but a perpendicular direction, a transversal movement that sweeps one *and* the other away, a stream without beginning or end that undermines its banks and picks up speed in the middle.
>
> *Deleuze & Guattari, 1987, p. 25*

Deleuze and Guattari built on philosopher Baruch Spinoza's concept of *common notion* to conceptualize the resulting composition when two or more things are brought into a relationship and create some *thing* independent of the things assembled (Phillips, 2006). According to philosopher Beth Lord (2010), Spinoza conceptualized the idea of *common notions* as "building blocks for rational knowledge"—a potential that is enhanced when bodies interact with bodies "of a similar nature" (p. 114). Of interest to diagrammatical thinkers is that for Spinoza what all things had in common was the capacity for infinite dynamism (Lord, 2010). Rather than look outside the objects or things brought into relationship and construct a category they both can share, the common attributes that matter in diagrammatical thinking is that all things exhibit states of "extended being . . . [which] contains within it all possible dynamic relations" (Lord, 2010, p. 42). The potential for "'infinite motion and rest' is the infinite set of variations of motion, which expresses all possible ways that physical beings can exist" (Lord, 2010, p. 42), that when combined create a dynamism that was not there before. For Deleuze (1988) the resulting composition is "an abstract machine . . . [that produces] a new kind of reality [and maps] relations between forces" (pp. 34–6). Literary scholar John Phillips provides an example to illustrate what this means:

The unity, for instance, of a poison and the body poisoned can be regarded as a state of becoming and an event which is reducible to neither the body nor the poison. The body and the poison, rather, participate in the event (which is what they have in common).

Phillips, 2006, p. 109

What social scientists working in diagrammatical modes of thinking seek is a way to work with this moving composition, this event, this "something whose mode of individuation is not that of a thing, but a hurricane or a battle— a becoming" (Bogue, 2004, pp. 77–8). The paradoxical nature of "becoming" —as something that is neither one nor the other or a combination of both—is believed to provide researchers with a way to talk about difference, and conceptualize its effects, without resorting to the limitations inherent in the other modes of thinking described.

What a focus on an "event" or "becoming" affords is a reconceptualization of a changing world that traverses common-place systems of meaning in ways that dissolve their usual connotations, and generate new thought-diagrams, or concepts (Colebrook, 2010). For example, feminist theorist Karen Barad (2007) creates the concept of "spacetimemattering" (p. 179) to argue that time, space, and matter cannot be usefully considered as separate, identifiable entities. Rather,

space, time, and matter are intra-actively produced in the ongoing differential articulation of the world. . . . The existence of the quantum discontinuity means that the past is never left behind, never finished once and for all, and the future is not what will come to be in an unfolding of the present moment; rather the past and the future are enfolded participants in matter's iterative becoming. Becoming is not an unfolding in time, but the inexhaustible dynamism of the enfolding of mattering.

Barad, 2007, p. 234

What is being articulated in approaches focused on assemblages (Deleuze & Guattari, 1987), actor-networks (Latour, 2005), cartographies (Guattari, 2013), and intra-active entanglements (Barad, 2007), to name a few, is a reconceptualization of all that has been previously assumed to reside in predetermined and separate domains (for example, psychologists study the human mind, geologists the earth, biologists living organisms, and each one is a disciplinary body of work distinct and separate from the other), to one of envisioning these domains in relations of "co-constitutive emergence" (Taylor, 2016, p. 208). Diagrammatical thinking might not be the best way to name this kind of thinking but I want to prioritize the idea of metamodeling as reading posited by Félix Guattari (2013), rather than the relationships that result from this reading, as these can fall prey too easily to static notions of networks and mappings. Literary critic Bruno Bosteels explains that this kind of reading,

> has to account for the multiple articulations of the social and the subject-ive, the material and the semiotic, between map and territory; it has to detect models to imagine how desire and production, madness and work, connect or intersect while cutting in and out of one another; it has to find ways to plot the lines of entwinement—both dense and ethereal, opaque and in your face for everyone to see—between knowledge and power, discourses and practices, between ways to see, to tell, and to make do, while scrupulously disentangling the tiniest knots; and it has to con-jecture how, between the real and the imaginary, or between the real and the symbolic, a precarious suture can take hold across the empty inter-stices, whereas in other instances a fissure rends apart the social surface all of a sudden to break the blissful spell of ready-made totalities.
>
> *Bosteels, 1998, p. 152*

Looking back at my study on parental involvement, how might diagram-matical thinking shift the study focus and design? What analytical questions would I have asked the data? What would the "data" consist of? As described in Chapter 4, dialectical thinking was the primary mode of thought used for that study. Therefore, in my analysis, I emphasized the contradictions and tensions between my data set and the discursive systems giving it shape. Diagrammatical thinking, on the contrary, seeks to disrupt both what is taken to be the content of reality and the processes through which this content has been framed. Malou Juelskjær (2013), drawing on Barad's work, explains that what is "produced through iterative intra-actions . . . [are materializations of] specific phenomena, where phenomena are not 'things' but relations" (p. 755). She revisits interview data collected as part of a longitudinal "study of 13-year-old students who changed schools to experience 'new beginnings'" (p. 754) to consider how an intra-active perspective alters her reading of one student's performed subjectivities. She first tells the story of Mary's enacted subjectivities from a poststructural perspective of multiple discursive positions, and then from an intra-active performative perspective. In the first, the interview is under-stood to produce a "specific 'present' in which Mary is positioned and positions herself within available discursive practices" (p. 760). In the second approach, however, Juelskjær makes sense of Mary's enacted subjectivities in relation to various shifting topologies. In other words, how her body performs "Mary" shifts continuously; a performed "dis/continuity" (p. 758), disrupting common notions of the self as an identifiable entity that reveals fragments of itself in response to different contexts.

How might Ellen or Lisa's stories or the concept of involvement as manifestations of the discourse on involvement be reconceptualized? What apparatuses would help them be thought of as performed "differences that matter" (Barad, 2007, p. 146)? Barad (2007) explains that apparatuses "are not merely assemblages that include nonhumans as well as humans. . . . [But] are boundary-making practices that are formative of matter and meaning, productive of, and part of, the phenomena produced" (pp. 142, 146). What boundary-making practices are revealed in the space between the concept of involvement and Ellen and Lisa's stories? Diagrammatical thinking pushes us to think of these stories as part of overlapping, but potentially different, topologies; as differentiable manifestations of performed "parentinvolvement" intersecting with other potentially modifying forces (for example, social class, knowledge, experience, affect, ecology, economy, personality, and so on). Parentinvolvement is not just some way to connect or combine parenting, schooling, and involvement but becomes something else altogether, something uniquely itself at the site of this juncture. Thinking diagrammatically pushes us to think of the way these, and other, concepts unfold and entwine as they affect everyday lives and practices. It helps us dissolve the illusionary divisions human disciplines have constructed in a way that reveals a relational materialism, an assembled ontology, previously hidden from view.

Characteristics of Diagrammatical Thinking

Dialectics is the art that invites us to recuperate alienated properties. Everything returns to the Spirit as the motor and product of the dialectic, or to self-consciousness, or even to man, as generic being. But if our properties in themselves express a diminished life and a mutilating thought, what is the use of recuperating them or becoming their true subject?

Deleuze, 2001, pp. 70–1

Seeking a way out of the impasse that dialectics is believed to create, Deleuze was one of the leading theorists proposing a different way of thinking; one that suggested that reading movement might allow humans to create themselves and their worlds differently. Thinking diagrammatically is challenging to visualize. Nevertheless, it offers a unique strategy that is different from the other four. What is being conceptualized is something that takes us beyond Venn diagrams or even complex maps; beyond notions of representation altogether. What makes it distinct is a focus on moving assemblages composed of human and nonhuman particles that should neither be conceptualized as identifiable parts linked together, nor as the result of a specific structural, discursive, or ideological framework. This is because diagrammatical thinking asks us to move away from conceptualizing things *as* something, or as something existing or identifiable, and think of objects, or parts of objects, as participating in an event of fast and slow moving assemblages: "becoming-mother" in one assemblage, "becoming-depression" in another, "becoming-matter" in a third, and so on. An "assemblage is a mode of ordering heterogeneous entities so that they work together for a certain time" (Müller, 2015, p. 28). For example, the poisoned body mentioned earlier is not some other manifestation of "poison" or "body," it is its own state; an emerging material presence affecting the event it is a part of. As political scientists Diana Coole and Samantha Frost (2010) explain, the emerging assemblages are "bodies composing their natural environment in ways that are corporeally meaningful for them, and subjectivities being constituted as open series of capacities or potencies that emerge hazardously and ambiguously within a multitude of organic and social processes" (p. 10). The assembled "diagram" stands outside of any notion of representation and, instead, "produces and creates, bringing new entities into existence and thereby serving an ontological function" (Watson, 2009, p. 11). It is "an arrangement that creates agency" (Müller, 2015, p. 28), and emphasizes the "processual character" of thought (Merrell, 1995, p. 51, as quoted in Semetsky, 2004, p. 436).

As with the descriptions of the other modes of thinking, the characteristics outlined here have been abstracted from multiple sources and may not be agreed upon by the theorists cited. Nevertheless, I believe that there are identifiable thinking strategies shared by theorists seeking to put into practice what I call diagrammatical thinking. Because of the radical shift in thinking required to understand this approach, an illustration is provided that I found helpful offered by philosopher Manuel DeLanda. DeLanda explains that conventional scientific thinking was based on a classification created by Aristotle who saw the world as

> populated by three categories of entities: *genus*, *species*, and *individual*. Entities belonging to the first two categories subsisted essentially, those belonging to the third one subsisted only accidentally. The genus could be, for example, Animal, the species Human, and the individual this or that particular person characterized by contingent properties: being white, being musical, being just. A genus was linked to its various species (Horse, Human) by a series of logically necessary subdivisions.
>
> *DeLanda, 2012, p. 220*

For example, he explains that humans and horses are both animals because they share characteristics that unite them as belonging to that *genus* or category, but they also have distinct characteristics which separate them into particular species or sub-categories. There is an undetermined range of individual variation within species, and, in turn, each species can be thought of as a variation of its overarching *genus*. Typically, when a new entity is discovered, the question is often what is this an instance of? To which existing category can this be added? As mentioned in Chapter 2 on categorical thinking, this process allows for categories themselves to be changed if the new entity makes visible previously unforeseen characteristics of a category. The issue for diagrammatical thinkers is that this kind of thinking merely reproduces one form of thought, which is not believed to be conducive to rethinking the world (Deleuze, 1995). To think differently requires thinking differently about the nature of things, and the relationship between things.

DeLanda's (2012) example provides a helpful entry point into this way of thinking. He shows that while it is rather easy to conceptualize that horses and humans belong to the same *genus* because of shared traits (that is, the categorical approach), it is much harder to conceptualize these on some sort of plane of transformational possibilities—a topological approach. DeLanda explains:

> What we need here is a means to conceptualize a "topological animal," an abstract animal that can become a human or a horse through a series of embryological operations: foldings, stretchings, invaginations, cellular migrations. . . . [I]f species must be conceived as *individual singularities*, genera must be replaced by a topological diagram structured by *universal singularities*.
>
> *DeLanda, 2012, p. 221*

Here the "abstract animal" should not be, and cannot be, thought of as an archetype containing preset variations of "animal," but as an "abstract machine" that operates independently from "the forms and substances, expressions and contents it will distribute" (Deleuze and Guattari, 1987, p. 141; see also Alliez, 2013). DeLanda explains that to understand how something like a diagram can animate transformation without being defined by what it animates, requires an understanding of the concept of "degrees of freedom." Degrees of freedom are

> the relevant ways in which a system is free to change. . . . Because as the degrees of freedom of a system change its overall state changes, a model of the system must capture the different possible states in which it can exist. . . . [T]his set of states may be represented as a *space of possibilities* with as many dimensions as the system has degrees of freedom.
>
> *DeLanda, 2012, pp. 221–2*

Although DeLanda explains that Deleuze and Guattari do not necessarily use these terms, and he goes into much more detail about their use of mathematical concepts than is relevant to my purpose, what is being conceptualized here is a way to consider the diagram as an articulation of matter and function (Deleuze and Guattari, 1987); an articulation that performs rather than explains. In other words, if we think of change on a moving continuum such as between a horse and human in an essentialist way, each splice in the continuum would be considered comparatively to some ideal feature (for example, is it more foot or hoof?), and in relation to some predetermined definition of "footness" or "hoofness." Thinking about this topologically removes essentialist categories from the picture altogether, as well as the idea that there is an actual continuous movement between foot and hoof. Instead each topological diagram itself is composed of these states of possibility, being neither foot nor hoof, but having the potential to become either, or branch out into another possible entity emerging from the topological space. This requires that researchers step away from part-whole conceptualizations of structure, or inductively- or deductively-derived logical conclusions, where language or other systems account for their conclusions, and turn to the analysis of assemblages in motion, which in the space of the possible can hypothetically be assemblages of an infinite number of possible arrangements.

This diagrammatical way of thinking has been used by mathematicians to speculate how multi-dimensional objects change when put into motion (Otte, 2011). Imagine, for example, a pyramid, which consists of several points, lines, and surfaces. In motion, the mathematical question becomes: What happens to these points, lines, and surfaces? (Otte, 2011). Similar to the horse to human example, an object or network of objects in motion will cause some of those lines, points, and surfaces to disintegrate, while new ones become not only possible, but likely. DeLanda's example should not cause us to think, however, that moving assemblages have identifiable beginnings or ends, or points in between. Even if one conceptualizes the movement from horse to human as a series of overlapping metamorphoses, such as the hoof to foot, hoof to hand, mane to hair, eye to eye, and so on, the variety of horse and human possibilities prevents any standardization. Every slice across continuums, therefore, cannot be considered to be inbetween one particular slice and the next, but has to be understood as its own state, a state *between* (Barad, 2010) non-definable, determined, or possible end points. Each slice is an enactment of a between-state, a state of becoming, a specific assemblage of matter and form that is something uniquely itself, neither the slice occurring before this one, nor the one occurring next. In this way, an assemblage, or state-space, is both an enactment of an individual singular *and* its topological structure. Each assembled entity, each event, "is always the index of a multiplicity" (Deleuze, 2001, p. 30), and is always "engaged in a process of actualization following the plane that gives it its particular reality" (Deleuze, 2001, p. 31). So although the degrees of freedom of the becoming-hoof, or some other state, might vary, they bring with them particular processes of actualization that, when combined, put into motion certain capacities or effects. Different combinations, such as adding poison or heat, would produce different effects, and so on.

Researchers working with diagrammatical modes of thinking are interested in how assemblages "emerge in particular ways, how they hold together, somewhat precariously, how they reach across or mould space and how they fall apart" (Müller, 2015, p. 27). Conceptualizing this process as a state-space, or "constellations of objects, bodies, expressions, qualities, and territories that come together" (Livesey, 2010, p. 18), and mapping its operations and effects, allows researchers to focus on the way human and nonhuman material entities evince a "self-organizing materiality . . . [generated through] the immanence of relations" (Braidotti, 2013, p. 82). DeLanda (2002) explains: "An individual may be characterized by a fixed number of definite properties (extensive and qualitative) and yet possess an *indefinite* number of capacities *to affect and be affected* by other individuals" (p. 62). In other words, the focus is on the "dynamic topological reconfigurings/entanglements/relationalities/(re)articulations" (Barad, 2007, p. 141) of the materializing assemblages formed among human, nonhuman, physical, or immaterial entities. The point here is to develop approaches that do not impose a perception of how things work or what things mean from the outside, but seek to understand their materializing effects from inside materialization itself; a materialization that never ceases to flow and change. In general, therefore, diagrammatical thinking:

1. *Consists of working with moving assemblages as open systems.* Assemblages are diagrams, topological compositions that are nonetheless vulnerable to interferences, resulting in unpredictable, but effect-producing paths.

> Assemblage can be seen as a relay concept, linking the problematic of structure with that of change and far-from-equilibrium systems. . . . It recognizes both structuring and indeterminate effects: that is, both flow and turbulence, produced in the interaction of open systems.
>
> *Venn, 2006, p. 107*

An assemblage is "composed of diverse elements and vibrant materials of all kinds" (de Freitas, 2012, p. 562). This means an assemblage is not a stable structure, but moving matter that collides, breaks apart, births new offshoots, connects with old conduits, or folds in new matter; its movement has often been compared to that of a rhizome (Deleuze & Guattari, 1987). Since it is always in the process of "becoming-other" (Bogue, 2010), a focus on assemblages is a focus on ontology, or "the problem of the way things exist for themselves and by themselves" (Stengers, 2011, pp. 373–4). In other words, diagrammatical thinking departs from the dialectical and its focus on oppositional tensions, and seeks, instead, to enter the fold (think of DeLanda's becoming-animal) as a way to articulate a movement of change without the usual dualities of inside/outside, below/above, ahead/behind. It is, as Deleuze and Guattari describe:

> a *map and not a tracing.* . . . What distinguishes the map from the tracing is that it is entirely oriented toward an experimentation in contact with the real. . . . The map is open and connectable in all of its dimensions; it is detachable, reversible, susceptible to constant modification. . . .

Perhaps one of the most important characteristics of the rhizome is that it always has multiple entry ways.

Deleuze & Guattari, 1987, p. 12

One of the tasks, therefore, for the researcher is to figure out how to enter this moving flow and work with this "ontology of becoming(s)" (Martin and Kamberelis, 2013, p. 670) in a way that produces new awareness of the effects of the flow, rather than naming it and, thus, reducing it to some concept outside of it. Becoming, therefore, is a tendency inherent to matter itself (Borradori, 2001); a potential intensity, or intense potential, manifesting itself at different points in time and in different relations. Furthermore, whereas dialectics presumes a specific movement for change, the result of tensions and fusions, the movement inherent to diagrammatical change is unpredictable, rhizomatic, chaotic even, in its randomness and openness to chance.

2. *Focuses on the performative event or agential operations of assembled entities.* The assemblage or diagram brings together *"relations of force"* (Alliez, 2013, p. 221), articulations of matter and function (Deleuze & Guattari, 1987). From a diagrammatical thinking perspective, "matter is not a formless blob that is given shape by our imaginings of it. It is not inert substance waiting to be discovered and described. It acts; matter pushes back. . . . Forces are produced. Momentum. Counterforces" (McCoy, 2012, p. 764). "Sense,"[2] therefore, however conceptualized—whether as "affect" (Deleuze, 1995; Deleuze & Guattari, 1987), "agency" (Latour, 2005; Barad, 2007), or some other concept— arises out of an arrangement of connections (Phillips, 2006). Vibrant relations enter the flux of change in ways "that open up new forms of life both for individuals and for collectives" (Martin & Kamberelis, 2013, p. 670). This means that matter is not something molded from the outside, but is itself "the condition that allows change, or life, as a constant movement of different- iation" (Borradori, 2001, p. 7). These relations open up lines of becoming that carry forward the capacity to act, while also being an enactment of that capacity. Furthermore, "power is not distributed evenly across the surface of an assemblage, since there are joints or nodes where there is more traffic and affect than at others" (de Freitas, 2012, p. 562). Rather, assemblages are sites of poten- tial, which open up possibilities for "new means of expression, a new territorial/ spatial organisation, a new institution, a new behaviour, or a new realisation" (Livesey, 2010, p. 19). Also, as sites of potential, an assemblage, or an event, can be a manifestation or materialization of any kind of agentic material and does not require a physical presence (Henriques, 2010). It is in this way that concepts need to be thought of as well. As Rebecca Coleman and Jessica Ringrose (2013) explain: "a concept is neither a pre-existing theoretical frame- work . . . nor a notion that springs from empirical research. . . . Rather, *concepts do things.* Understanding concepts as *doing* is, fundamentally, an understanding of concepts as becoming" (p. 8).

In this sense concepts *are* becomings. For example, a concept such as mobility is itself a doing that transforms. It is not a concept one is applying perhaps to a social class group to discuss what that group is doing, but is itself a part of this assemblage. Similarly, theory is itself practice, and both (although there is no real differentiation between the two) produce effects *as* things, not *to* things. The focus is not on the one thing or the other thing it becomes, but on *that* which transforms it; that is, the line of becoming. Transformations have multiple, connecting, disconnecting, transversing lines, and so on. The diagram, then, both maps the function of the moving arrangement (Livesey, 2010), and is the "abstract machine [that] makes things happen" (Cole, 2012, p. 12). Figure 6.1 illustrates the idea of a phenomenon becoming through articulations of matter and function.

3. Is creative, interventionist, and experimental. Theorists who use diagrammatical strategies view research as an intervention and the world as a vast arena of, and for, ongoing experimentation. However, what this means conceptually or practically is difficult to pin down. Philosopher Ian Hacking (1982) explains that we cannot "know" reality or "see" what it is made up of, but we can manipulate reality in ways that make visible the interconnecting parts. Using the example of electrons, he states: "The 'direct' proof of electrons and the like is our ability to manipulate them using well understood low-level causal properties. . . . Hence, *engineering*, not theorizing, is the proof of scientific realism about entities" (p. 86, my emphasis). Thinking about the world using Spinoza's notion of infinite dynamism, reveals a world made up of a wide variety of states of rest and motion, ranging from moments of calm to chaotic

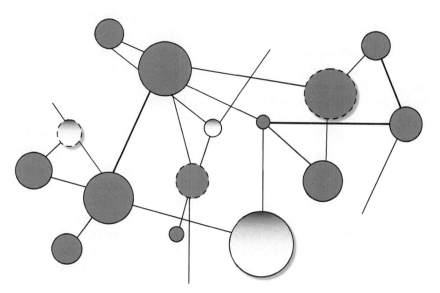

FIGURE 6.1   A Phenomenon Becoming

turbulences. While not always visible, these states of rest and motion participate in making the world visible in different ways and, when combined with others, put into motion an infinite range of potential states.

Elaborating on the development of "a nonrepresentationalist realist account of scientific practices that takes the material nature of practices seriously," Barad (2007) argues that "theorizing and experimenting are not about *intervening* (from outside) but about *intra-acting* from within . . . the phenomena produced" (p. 56). One way of understanding this is that as we participate in the flow of matter, and produce what matters, we are always engaging in experimentation and creating turbulences that intervene wherever we go. Experimentation is "a way to intervene, not a theory of what to think" (Fenwick & Edwards, 2010, p. 1) and, through intervention we, along with other materializing agents, bring phenomena into existence (Hacking, 1982). DeLanda explains this well:

> In learning by doing, or by interacting with and adjusting to materials, machines and models, experimentalists *progressively discern* what is relevant and what is not in a given experiment. In other words, the distribution of the important and the unimportant defining an experimental problem (what degrees of freedom matter, what disturbances do not make a difference) are not grasped at a glance . . . but [are] slowly brought to light as the assemblage stabilizes itself through the mutual accommodation of its heterogeneous components. In this assemblage the singularities and affects of the experimentalist's body are meshed with those of machines, models and material processes in order for learning to occur and for embodied expertise to accumulate.
>
> *DeLanda, 2002, pp. 143–4*

4. *Is anti-reductionist.* As mentioned earlier, a moving assemblage frozen at any point in time is always a unique configuration carrying forward an enactment of a unique singularity *and* the structuring plane or system of operation giving shape to its operational capacity. It is, therefore, always an enactment of difference, of multiplicity. What is being conceptualized here is "difference-in-itself" (Cole, 2012, p. 5). Here the concept of difference is no longer the dialectical "other," the assumed *anti*-thesis. Whereas dialectics conceptualizes difference by negation (that is, something is an "a" only because it is not a "non-a") (Borradori, 2001, p. 3), difference-in-itself is internal to itself and "implies something like a shade, a nuance" (Borradori, 2001, p. 3). Similarly to poetical thinking, difference multiplies: "The virtual insensible matter becomes intelligible . . . [in its] capacity to awaken the virtual or potential multiplicities that are implicit in any surface" (de Freitas & Sinclair, 2012, p. 141). It is for this reason that researchers working with diagrammatical modes of thinking talk about assemblages as non-reproducible and non-representational. As Deleuze and Guattari (1987) assert: "The multiple *must be made*" (p. 6).

Diagrammatical Thinking in Practice

Diagrammatical thinking radically alters the focus and nature of social science research. Working from the assumption that reality is already performing assemblages, materializing relationships, and creating some sort of order out of chaos (Prigogine & Stengers, 1984), it brings to the analytic task a way of reading, or a form of intervening, into this moving matter. Like researchers drawing on poetical thinking strategies, researchers working in diagrammatical modes are deeply "entangled within the assemblages they seek to study" (Coleman & Ringrose, 2013, p. 6). However, unlike poetical thinking which opens an aesthetic relation between world and humans, diagrammatical entanglements are more complex as neither human nor object takes precedence in the direction taken by materializing assemblages. This is because it is neither

> an object or subject that becomes—indeed there is no subject of becoming or a thing that is the result of becoming—but only something in objects and subjects that transforms them and makes them other than what they used to be.
>
> *Grosz, 2011, p. 51*

Researchers working with diagrammatical thinking strategies, therefore, seek ways to find this "something in objects and subjects" and through materializing assemblages study their transformational effects. They do this by focusing on events, "agential intra-actions" (Barad, 2007), "lines of flight and intensities" (Deleuze & Guattari, 1987, p. 4), "ordinary affects" (Stewart, 2007), and other spaces of intensive potentialities where things or "thinking might happen" (Colebrook, 2010, p. 2).

Julian Henriques' (2010) study of affect offers a different way of reading the propagation of affect and is a good example of diagrammatical thinking. As anthropologist Kathleen Stewart (2007) explains from a diagrammatical perspective: "Ordinary affects are the varied, surging capacities to affect and to be affected that give everyday life the quality of a continual motion of relations, scenes, contingencies, and emergences. They're things that happen" (pp. 1–2). As a result, she states, their analysis is not straightforward; "they have to be mapped through different, coexisting forms of composition, habituation, and event" (Stewart, 2007, p. 4). This is what Henriques (2010) sets out to do. By analyzing how "affect is expressed rhythmically—through relationships, reciprocations, resonances, syncopations and harmonies . . . [he sought to enact] a vibrant cultural studies, working and thinking through vibrations themselves, rather than a cultural studies of vibration" (p. 58).

Henriques argues that affect does not preexist the situation, but arises out of the event, while also being a crucial component of its propagation. This is not, therefore, a study of a dancehall, or of musicians' or dancers' perceptions of affect. Rather, it is a study of the concept of affect itself. And it is in the "propagation of vibrations" (Henriques, 2010, p. 58) or, in this case, sound waves, that the intensity and texture of this concept is revealed. To do this, Henriques uses three procedures—counting, measuring, and listening—to discuss socio-cultural, corporeal, and material sound waves as affect in a dancehall scene. Briefly, counting focuses on rhythm, pitch, interactions, and so on; measuring focuses on a consideration of the value and amplitude of the sonic experience; and listening seeks out the tone or "timbre" of the event—"its distinctive quality, the details that make one night different from another" (p. 60). He asserts that this model "offers an organizing principle for the transmission of affect—that eludes the prism of representation—and for the meaning of affect—that escapes the prison house of language" (p. 83). Inquiry, such as this, is inventive in that it participates in the movement of becoming, dislodging the hold that language and reason has had on science, showing the way concepts such as affect might produce a choreographed effect by "riding these sound waves" (Henriques, 2010, p. 66). He concludes: "Breaking the boundaries of text, image and the surfaces of objects, vibrations offer an opportunity to conceptualize the permeability of individuals in their environment as they selectively transduce and amplify its energetic patterns—that is, propagate affect" (p. 84).

Researchers working in diagrammatical modes of thinking are just as concerned with human issues as researchers working in other modes. However, as is evident from the characteristics outlined, the inclusion of human voices in research is done differently and aims to produce different effects. Emma Renold and Jessica Ringrose's (2008) study on girls and gender provides another example of the way in which human perspectives and conceptual analyses are intertwined to produce new designs for research. As feminist researchers working with diagrammatical approaches they sought ways to conduct research on concepts such as gender formation outside of the assumed male-female binary. They argue that while there has been much critical work done on the intersections of gender, cultural representation, and the way in which girls resist or negotiate dominant and privileged conceptions of heterosexuality, like others resisting a dialectical concept of resistance as an either/or, they seek a way *into* "the micro complexities that reveal girls as at once reinscribing and disrupting the postfeminist terrain that demands hypersexualized femininities" (p. 315). In order to do this, they revisit data collected in two separate studies (one an ethnographic study of preteen "boys' and girls' constructions of sex/gender/sexuality" (p. 320), the other narrative interview data of young teenage girls' friendship groups) as a way to think differently about "how girls are living and performing 'girl'" (p. 320). By reading the two data sets through multiple lenses and tracing how different resources were brought together or subverted by the girls, Renold and Ringrose provide an analysis of how the girls can be said to simultaneously inhabit and resist the heteronormative and hypersexualized discourses and behaviors in ways that show resistance and rupture without necessarily escaping the hold they have on them. They conclude by calling for new approaches to the "analysis of resistance and subversion within (not escape from) the regulatory force of the heterosexual matrix" (p. 333).

What these examples demonstrate is that researchers moving away from dialectical, categorical, or narrative thinking seek ways to work the generative potential of a distinct event formed at the junctures of a moving assemblage. As in other modes of thinking, possibilities for diagrammatical research are vast. However what seems clear from the examples provided is that researchers interested in putting it to work are considering new and innovative ways of assembling the available and not-yet-imagined heterogeneous entities and, as such, are responding in unique ways to Patti Lather and Elizabeth St. Pierre's (2013) question: "How do we think a 'research problem' in the imbrication of an agentic assemblage of diverse elements that are constantly intra-acting, never stable, never the same?" (p. 630).

Deciding on Diagrammatical Thinking for Analysis

In his book, *After method: Mess in social science research*, sociologist John Law writes:

> What does this mean in practice? The answer is that I do not know. But one thing is indeed clear. In the longer run it is no longer obvious that the disciplines and the research fields of science and social science are appropriate in their present form. . . . [W]e need quite other metaphors for imagining our worlds and our responsibilities to those worlds. Localities. Specificities. Enactments. Multiplicities. Fractionalities. Goods. Resonances. Gatherings. Forms of craftings. Processes of weaving. Spirals. Vortices. Indefiniteness. Condensates. Dances. Imaginaries. Passions. Interferences. . . . Metaphors for the stutter and the stop. Metaphors for quiet and more generous versions of method.
>
> *Law, 2004, p. 156*

Given the level of uncertainties and complexities involved in rethinking social sciences and the world, why choose a diagrammatical lens for research? The first reason is that diagrammatical modes of thinking are meant to help conceptualize difference differently. Difference is not determined by what something is or is not, but is enacted in the event of becoming (Coleman & Ringrose, 2013; Deleuze & Guattari, 1987; Derrida & Stiegler, 2002; Masny, 2013). A focus on difference as becoming, as a multiplicity, provides a way to step out of dominant forms of thinking (such as dialectics), which are perceived to create an impasse in that the very way of thinking about research predetermines what will be found (Deleuze, 1995). To break out of this quagmire requires a reconceptualization of the very concepts that make up philosophy. Claire

Colebrook (2010) states: "A philosopher's concepts produce connections and styles of thinking. Concepts are intensive: they do not gather together an already existing set of things (extension); they allow for movements and connection" (p. 1). From a diagrammatical perspective, "the event is a disruption, violence or dislocation of thinking" (Colebrook, 2010, p. 4). Research, as an example of such an event, can participate in the dethroning of preconceived ways of seeing and doing. Researchers using diagrammatical thinking seek to successfully disrupt established hierarchies such as assuming that only humans have agency, and demonstrate that all matter possesses "its own mode of self-transformation, self-organization, and directedness" (Coole & Frost, 2010, p. 10). Diagrammatical approaches give researchers "new ways to capture the agency that new forms of materiality afford" (Pinch, 2008, p. 478).

Second, and related, understanding difference to be an enactment of moving assemblages (or as "dispersions of the subject," Foucault, 1972a, p. 55) helps to rearticulate an understanding of change as discordant, discontinuous, and random, rather than ordered, continuous, and purposeful (Barad, 2010). And, so again, stepping away from pre-established ways of seeing and understanding shifts ways of thinking about the world from the perspective of identification or emplotment to one where affects, agency, and change emanate from multiple intersecting diagrams, topologies, and assemblages (Barad, 2007; Coleman & Ringrose, 2013; Latour, 2005; Müller, 2015). This requires discarding traditional notions of matter and how matter has been delineated. Diagrammatically, human bodies and objects are made up of particles that exist in the world and perform their existence in a variety of ways. In other words, the analytic work is not to look for commonalities, or plot the points into representations of an existing or perceived reality, or synthesize contradictory viewpoints into new understandings. The point of diagrammatical thinking is to acknowledge human materiality alongside other matter and enter into co-constituting relationships in ways that put into motion new continuums of becoming for humans, nonhumans, institutions, material and conceptual entities, and their infinite and possible intersections. Feminist scholars Carol Taylor and Gabrielle Ivinson (2013) explain: "This post-human ethic of 'worlding' is not a matter of choice, will or intent but a matter of our 'incarnate relation' that precedes consciousness and individualism, borne of our being in and of the world" (p. 667).

Third, choosing diagrammatical thinking provides a way to rethink research as an event, a site of creative experimentation (Masny, 2013). Diagrammatical thinking is generative, turning preconceptualized entities on their heads, stretching them in new ways, folding them into one another in the creation of new concepts. "*Theorizing, like experimenting, is a material practice*" (Barad, 2007, p. 55). In this way, traditional qualitative strategies such as interviewing, working with documents, or coding are being rethought and re-imagined. Of coding, MacLure (2013) writes: "Perhaps we could think of coding, then, as just such an experiment with order and disorder, in which provisional and partial taxonomies are formed, but are always subject to change and metamorphosis, as new connections spark among words, bodies, objects and ideas" (p. 181).

In general, then, diagrammatical thinking helps researchers:

- Reconceptualize interactions (human and nonhuman) as transversal forces without foundations or predetermined aims
- Disrupt established forms of thinking
- Engineer new articulations of the effects of turbulent encounters between diverse human and nonhuman particles

There are numerous challenges to reconceptualizing research in diagrammatical ways. First, similarly to dialectical and poetical approaches, diagrammatical approaches are inherently subversive. Researchers using diagrammatical approaches assume that all research is political and affects the way the world is read, understood, and researched. It is for this reason that these approaches seek to enter in the midst of change, reworking its possibilities and directions. "Unpacking the affective flows in a research-assemblage both reveals its micropolitics, and provides the means to re-engineer a research-assemblage or research machine to manipulate its affect economy and thereby its micropolitics" (Fox & Alldred, 2014, p. 13).

Second, re-engineering the world requires not only a different kind of reading, but a different language, set of concepts, and use of metaphors. MacLure explains:

> We need new metaphors of the relation between researchers and subjects, such as entanglement, knots, weaves and tissues . . . metaphors of *fabrication* in other words. . . . Derrida (1981) reminds us that the words 'text', 'tissue' and 'textile' have a common etymology, and the weaver's creations—webs, nets, meshes, knots, threads, membranes, gauzes, tissues—run through his work as figures of Writing. Life-history researchers (like any other researchers) and their subjects (like any other subjects) produce *text*. Their accounts are always fabrications . . . weaving something new, yet assembled out of fragments and recollections of other fabrications.
>
> *MacLure, 2003, p. 127*

These new metaphors and concepts can result in people finding the language and theories guiding these approaches difficult to understand, and, thus, exclusionary and alienating. As a result, the language itself risks leaving the intended audience, whether these are people affected by the research or other researchers, frustrated or unaffected by the results of the research (Greene, 2013).

Additionally, adopting diagrammatical modes of thinking does not eliminate the usual range of concerns regarding meaning and representation, of which I will mention two. The first issue is how to account for the "human" in modes of thinking that embrace a "posthumanist" ontology. "Posthumanism is the historical moment that marks the end of the opposition between Humanism and anti-humanism and traces a different discursive framework, looking more affirmatively towards new alternatives" (Braidotti, 2013, p. 37), especially in seeking "alternative ways of conceptualizing the human subject" (Braidotti, 2013, p. 37). However, what is happening in some cases, according to Kay Anderson and Colin Perrin, is that researchers drawing on diagrammatical theories seem to be dismissing the human altogether, rather than accounting for their effects (physical and spiritual) as a material entity. In their words:

> It is . . . according to a classical ontological dualism—in which the defin-
> ing characteristic of the human (as essentially immaterial) is separated
> from the nonhuman (defined as irremediably material)—that humanism
> has come to be understood as an 'immaterialism'. Identified with the
> belief that the human mind is ontologically distinct (and not—as for
> materialism generally—simply reducible to biology), human exceptional-
> ism is rejected as escapist fantasy. What we want to argue here, however,
> is that this critique of humanism constitutes something of a blind spot for
> the claim—which we share—that 'everything is material' (Coole and
> Frost 9). For if *everything* is material, wouldn't the 'fantasy' of human
> exceptionality also have to be considered a 'material configuration'?
> And, as such, wouldn't *its* 'distinctive capacities or efficacious
> powers' need to be treated as a 'worldly'—rather than an 'otherworldly'
> —construction?
>
> *Anderson & Perrin, 2015, p. 3*

As Braidotti's quote above suggests, the intention of posthumanism is not to eliminate the human subject but to reconsider altogether the idea of the subject. Therefore, one challenge of working with diagrammatical modes is how to account for human materiality in ways that do not reconstruct a preconceived embodiment or erase effects and traces left by humans altogether.

Second, scholars taking up diagrammatical strategies have been criticized for providing general critiques from which "to authorize new terrain" (Ahmed, 2008, p. 33), and then creating concepts that suggest a "return to old binaries— between nature/materiality/biology and culture in the very argument that 'matter' is what is missing from feminist work" (Ahmed, 2008, p. 34). Diagrammatical thinkers, therefore, should be mindful of the language used and the way in which their concepts might be reproducing a landscape similar to the one they are criticizing.

In addition to issues of language and representation, diagrammatical approaches reject the separation of quantitative and qualitative methodologies, the natural and social sciences, and other divisions that are no longer considered valid modes of organization. Choosing diagrammatical thinking, therefore, requires a commitment to dig into a complex and interdisciplinary body of literature and a willingness to become "better equipped to deal with mess, confusion and relative disorder" (Law, 2004, p. 2).

Notes

1 Diagrammatical thinking should not be confused with diagrammatic reasoning involving "*diagrams* as a means for representation and processing of knowledge" (Kulpa, 2009, p. 75), or a form of spatial reasoning depicting relationships (Byrne & Johnson-Laird, 1989) in the sense of "thinking diagrammatically [to create] visual forms of information and knowledge transfer" (Saldaña, 2015, p. 147) as in the construction of maps and figures.
2 In French, sense or *sens*, refers to meaning as well as direction (Phillips, 2006).

References

Ahmed, S. (2008). Imaginary prohibitions: Some preliminary remarks on the founding gestures of the 'new materialism.' *European Journal of Women's Studies, 15*(1), 23–39.

Alliez, É. (2013). Ontology of the diagram and biopolitics of philosophy. A research programme on transdisciplinarity. *Deleuze Studies, 7*(2), 217–30.

Anderson, K., & Perrin, C. (2015). New Materialism and the stuff of humanism. *Australian Humanities Review, 58*, 1–15.

Barad, K. (2007). *Meeting the universe halfway: Quantum physics and the entanglement of matter and meaning.* Durham, NC: Duke University Press.

Barad, K. (2010). Quantum entanglements and hauntological relations of inheritance: Dis/continuities, spacetime enfoldings, and justice-to-come. *Derrida Today, 3*(2), 240–68.

Bijker, W. E., & Law, J. (Eds.) (1992). *Shaping technology/building society: Studies in sociotechnical change.* Cambridge, MA: The MIT Press.

Bogue, R. (1989). *Deleuze and Guattari.* London: Routledge.

Bogue, R. (2004). *Deleuze's wake: Tributes and tributaries.* Albany, NY: State University of New York Press.

Bogue, R. (2010). *Deleuzian fabulation and the scars of history.* Edinburgh, UK: Edinburgh University Press.

Borradori, G. (2001). The temporalization of difference: Reflections on Deleuze's interpretation of Bergson. *Continental Philosophy Review, 34*, 1–20.

Bosteels, B. (1998). 'From text to territory: Félix Guattari's cartography of the unconscious.' In E. Kaufman & K. J. Heller (Eds.), *Deleuze & Guattari: New mappings in politics, philosophy, and culture* (pp. 145–74). Minneapolis, MN: University of Minnesota Press.

Braidotti, R. (2013). *The posthuman.* Malden, MA: Polity Press.

Byrne, R. M. J., & Johnson-Laird, P. N. (1989). Spatial reasoning. *Memory and Language, 28*(5), 564–75.

Cole, D. R. (2012). Matter in motion: The educational materialism of Gilles Deleuze. *Educational Philosophy and Theory*, *44*(S1), 3–17.

Colebrook, C. (2010). 'Introduction.' In A. Parr (Ed.), *The Deleuze dictionary revised edition* (pp. 1–6). Edinburgh, UK: Edinburgh University Press.

Coleman, R., & Ringrose, J. (2013). 'Introduction: Deleuze and research methodologies.' In Coleman, R. & Ringrose, J. (Eds.), *Deleuze and research methodologies* (pp. 1–22). Edinburgh, UK: Edinburgh University Press.

Coole, D., & Frost, S. (2010). 'Introducing the new materialisms.' In D. Coole and S. Frost (Eds.), *New materialisms: Ontology, agency, and politics* (pp. 1–43). Durham, NC: Duke University Press.

de Freitas, E. (2012). The classroom as rhizomes: New strategies for diagramming knotted interactions. *Qualitative Inquiry*, *18*(7), 557–70.

de Freitas, E., & Sinclair, N. (2012). Diagram, gesture, agency: Theorizing embodiment in the mathematics classroom. *Educational Studies in Mathematics*, *80*(1–2), 133–52.

DeLanda, M. (2002). *Intensive science and virtual philosophy*. New York, NY: Continuum.

DeLanda, M. (2012). 'Deleuze, mathematics, and realist ontology.' In D. W. Smith and H. Somers-Hall (Eds.), *The Cambridge companion to Deleuze* (pp. 220–38). Cambridge, UK: Cambridge University Press.

Deleuze, G. (1988). *Foucault* (edited and trans. by Seán Hand). Minneapolis, MN: University of Minnesota Press (originally published in French, 1986).

Deleuze, G. (1995). *Difference & repetition* (trans. by Paul Patton). New York, NY: Columbia University Press (originally published in French, 1968).

Deleuze, G. (2001). *Pure immanence: Essays on a life* (trans. by A. Boyman and with introduction by J. Rajchman). New York, NY: Zone Books.

Deleuze, G., & Guattari, F. (1987). *A thousand plateaus: Capitalism and schizophrenia* (trans. by Brian Massumi). Minneapolis, MN: University of Minnesota Press (originally published in French, 1980).

Derrida, J. (1981). *Dissemination* (trans. by B. Johnson). London: Athlone Press.

Derrida, J., & Stiegler, B. (2002). *Echographies of television: Filmed interviews* (trans. by Jennifer Bajorek). Cambridge, UK: Polity Press.

Fenwick, T., & Edwards, R. (2010). *Actor-network theory in education*. New York, NY: Routledge.

Foucault, M. (1972a). *The archaeology of knowledge and the discourse on language* (trans. by A. M. Sheridan Smith). New York, NY: Pantheon Books.

Fox, N. J., & Alldred, P. (2014): New materialist social inquiry: Designs, methods and the research-assemblage. *International Journal of Social Research Methodology*. (DOI: 10.1080/13645579.2014.921458).

Genosko, G. (2001). 'Introduction.' In G. Genosko (Ed.), *Deleuze and Guattari: Critical assessments of leading philosophers* (pp. 1–13). New York, NY: Routledge.

Greene, J. C. (2013). On rhizomes, lines of flight, mangles, and other assemblages. *International Journal of Qualitative Studies in Education*, *26*(6), 749–58.

Grosz, E. (2011). *Becoming undone: Darwinian reflections on life, politics, and art*. Durham, NC: Duke University Press.

Guattari, F. (2013). *Schizoanalytic cartographies* (trans. by Andrew Goffey). London: Bloomsbury Academic (originally published in French, 1989).

Hacking, I. (1982). Experimentation and scientific realism. *Philosophical Topics*, *13*(1), 71–87.

Henriques, J. (2010). The vibrations of affect and their propagation on a night out on Kingston's dancehall scene. *Body & Society, 16*(1), 57–89.

Juelskjær, M. (2013). Gendered subjectivities of spacetimematter. *Gender and Education, 25*(6), 754–68.

Kulpa, Z. (2009). Main problems of diagrammatic reasoning. Part I: The generalization problem. *Foundations of Science, 14,* 75–96.

Lather, P., and St. Pierre, E. A. (2013). Introduction: Post-qualitative research. *International Journal of Qualitative Studies in Education, 26*(6), 629–33.

Latour, B. (2005). *Reassembling the social: An introduction to actor-network-theory.* Oxford, UK: Oxford University Press.

Law, J. (2004). *After method: Mess in social science research.* New York, NY: Routledge.

Livesey, G. (2010). 'Assemblage.' In A. Parr (Ed.), *The Deleuze dictionary* (rev. edn., pp. 18–19). Edinburgh, UK: Edinburgh University Press.

Lord, B. (2010). *Spinoza's ethics: An Edinburgh philosophical guide.* Edinburgh, UK: Edinburgh University Press.

MacLure, M. (2003). *Discourse in educational and social research.* Philadelphia, PA: Open University Press.

MacLure, M. (2013). 'Classification or wonder? Coding as an analytic practice in qualitative research.' In R. Coleman & J. Ringrose (Eds.), *Deleuze and research methodologies* (pp. 164–83). Edinburgh, UK: Edinburgh University Press.

Martin, A. D., & Kamberelis, G. (2013). Mapping not tracing: Qualitative educational research with political teeth. *International Journal of Qualitative Studies in Education, 26*(6), 668–79.

Masny, D. (2013). Rhizoanalytic pathways in qualitative research. *Qualitative Inquiry, 19*(5), 339–48.

McCoy, K. (2012). Toward a methodology of encounters: Opening to complexity in qualitative research. *Qualitative Inquiry, 18*(9), 762–72.

Müller, M. (2015). Assemblages and actor-networks: Rethinking socio-material power, politics and space. *Geography Compass, 9*(1), 27–41.

Otte, M. (2011). Space, complementarity, and "diagrammatic reasoning." *Semiotica, 186*(1/4), 275–96.

Phillips, J. (2006). Agencement/assemblage. *Theory, Culture & Society, 23*(2–3), 108–9.

Pinch, T. (2008). Technology and institutions: Living in a material world. *Theory and Society, 37*(5), 461–83.

Prigogine, I., & Stengers, I. (1984). *Order out of chaos: Man's new dialogue with nature.* London: William Heinemann.

Renold, E., & Ringrose, J. (2008). Regulation and rupture: Mapping tween and teenage girls' resistance to the heterosexual matrix. *Feminist Theory, 9*(3), 313–38.

Saldaña, J. (2015). *Thinking qualitatively: Methods of mind.* Thousand Oaks, CA: Sage.

Semetsky, I. (2004). The role of intuition in thinking and learning: Deleuze and the pragmatic legacy. *Educational Philosophy and Theory, 36*(4), 433–54.

Stengers, I. (2011). 'Wondering about materialism.' In L. Bryant, N. Srnicek, & G. Harman (Eds.), *The speculative turn: Continental materialism and realism* (pp. 368–80). Melbourne, AU: re.press.

Stewart, K. (2007). *Ordinary affects.* Durham, NC: Duke University Press.

Taylor, C. A., & Ivinson, G. (2013). Material feminisms: New direction for education. *Gender and Education, 25*(6), 665–70.

Taylor, C. A. (2016). Close encounters of a critical kind: A diffractive musing in/ between new material feminism and object-oriented ontology. *Cultural Studies <=> Critical Methodologies, 16*(2), 201–12.

Venn, C. (2006). A note on assemblage. *Theory, Culture & Society, 23*(2–3), 107–8.

Watson, J. (2009). *Guattari's diagrammatic thought: Writing between Lacan and Deleuze.* London, UK: Continuum.

7
TEACHING QUALITATIVE ANALYSIS

Thinking is not something 'we' do; thinking happens to us, from without. There is a *necessity* to thinking, for the event of thought lies beyond the autonomy of choice. Thinking happens.

Claire Colebrook, 2002, p. 38

History shows that everything that has been thought will be thought again by a thought that does not yet exist.

Michel Foucault, 1970, p. 372

I began this book with a call to attend to the diversity of thinking strategies at play in qualitative research. After providing an extensive analysis of strategic actions in a wide range of situations, Freedman (2013) wonders about the utility of a term that has become synonymous with planning. He states: "It is hard to avoid the conclusion that while strategy is undoubtedly a good thing to have, it is a hard thing to get right" (p. 608). He concludes:

So what turns something that is not quite strategy into strategy is a sense of actual or imminent instability, a changing context that induces a sense of conflict. Strategy therefore starts with an existing state of affairs and only gains meaning by an awareness of how, for better or worse, it could be different.

Freedman, 2013, p. 611

I believe that what Freedman describes is a good description of analysis and, I hope, your experience in reading this book. For example, in reading the descriptions of each mode of thinking many questions must have arisen, especially when considering my typology in relation to methodological and theoretical distinctions already made in the qualitative literature. Isn't grounded theory both categorical and narrative? Is phenomenology primarily approached from a narrative or poetical perspective? In what way do the modes of thinking map onto distinctions made between interpretive, critical, poststructural, and other paradigms (Lather, 2006; Prasad, 2005)? I am also sure that when considering their applicability to your own research you found yourself drawn to some aspects of each, while discarding others. So, another question which might be entertained is whether the modes of thinking can be mixed and, if so, how?

Like Freedman, I believe strategies form in response to instability. I also believe that they gain credibility when they are considered or applied with knowledge of the competing systems of meaning that give them shape. My inspiration for writing this book was the belief that it is difficult to do credible analysis, or to imagine new design configurations for research, if unaware of the underpinnings of your chosen approach and of its relation to other theoretical and methodological options available within the field of qualitative research. My intention was to identify and describe distinct modes of thinking that have made a difference to how data, knowledge, and meaning have been conceptualized and defined. Frederick Erickson (2011) explains that qualitative researchers are interested in inquiring about "meaning-relevant *kinds* of things in the world— kinds of people, kinds of actions, kinds of beliefs and interests—focusing on differences in forms of things that make a difference for meaning" (p. 43), including, I would add, inquiry approaches that extend beyond meaning itself.

Furthermore, strategies are not just actions that stand outside beliefs about the world. While there are always limitations to organizational approaches such as the one used in this book, I believe that I have successfully demonstrated how the distinct assumptions, actions, aims, and language of each mode of thinking create a strategy for analysis whose use cannot be considered without also taking into account these fundamental characteristics. Certainly, as has been argued, strategies such as categorizing, narrating, diagramming, and so on, are made use of within many modes of thinking in a variety of ways. However, I would also argue that, when mixed they become something else, and require consideration for how, and why, they are being brought together.

As mentioned in Chapter 1, "mode of thinking" has been used as a way to analyze the thinking strategies that distinguish one theoretical perspective from another without, for the most part, defining these in relation to those theoretical perspectives. The reason given in the Introduction is that many qualitative approaches can be carried out from different epistemological orientations and so using broad umbrella terms, such as narrative inquiry, can be confusing especially when seeking guidance for analysis. However, another reason is simply that the terminology itself—terms such as "theoretical perspective," "methodology," or "theory,"[1]— are not used consistently to mean the same thing. Showing the workings of each mode of thinking, rather than defining them as in, for example, a critical or interpretivist approach, not only illustrates how theories such as phenomenology or critical theory might be carried out in practice, it also provides flexibility for the strategies to be used and named in a variety of ways to support the design formations they might become a part of.

By focusing on the strategies themselves, I was able to reveal the theoretical assumptions that have given them shape in a way that demonstrates that while strategies can, and will, be mixed, doing so without understanding their unique history, aim, and effect runs the risk of carrying out a superficial bricolage (Kincheloe, 2001). Bricolage involves "the making do and 'artisan-like inventiveness' (De Certeau 1984: xviii) by which actors produce their own intentful activities from the practices that structure everyday activity" (Jarzabkowski, 2004, pp. 544–5). To avoid superficiality in an interdisciplinary discipline such as qualitative research,

> scholars would study the social construction of the discipline's knowledge bases, epistemologies, and knowledge production methodologies. As scholars analyzed the historical origins of the field, they would trace the emergence of various schools of thought, conflicts within the discipline, and the nature and effects of paradigmatic changes.
>
> *Kincheloe, 2001, pp. 683–4*

So while advocating for bricolage, a methodological entanglement that is already underway (Kincheloe, 2001), I worry that, in the midst of arguments being simultaneously forwarded in support of paradigmatic mixing (Greene & Hall, 2010), and new empirical entanglements that are rewriting the world (Coole & Frost, 2010), the very distinctions that have served to construct the diversity inherent to the field of qualitative research, and the political and practical divisions and alliances this diversity has spawned, are not being adequately addressed in introductory research courses. As mentioned in Chapter 1, courses in the Qualitative Research Program at the University of Georgia work with this diversity, finding strength in the cross-disciplinary conversations of students, and the interdisciplinary and multi-paradigmatic nature of our discipline. Furthermore, as Judith Preissle (2011) explains, our students "are the future. To produce and to respond to what is to come, they need as much of the qualitative resources provided by others as we can manage" (p. 693).

A core challenge for those who teach and conduct qualitative analysis is the sheer magnitude of analytical and theoretical choices on which to draw. And, while no individual, or text, can even begin to make a dent in introducing this field, this diversity has to be taught regardless of the instructor's analytical preferences. This does not mean, however, taking a neutral stance on what is taught. On the contrary, I, like other instructors, bring a particular stance to the "qualitative pedagogy" (Preissle & deMarrais, 2011) that guides my teaching. For example, I agree with Joe Kincheloe (2001) about the need to foster a critical and reflexive form of "boundary work" (p. 689). As such my teaching is deeply influenced by hermeneutics; the theory of the study of interpretation, and quintessential theory of translation and mediation between realms, whatever those realms might be (Palmer, 1980). Here I describe some of the core concepts that have shaped my teaching, namely: diversity, tradition, reflexivity, dialogue, and practice.

On Diversity

The issue of diversity poses a dilemma for social scientists. To think of anything as different always requires, it seems, a thinking of something from which difference emanates, which invariably reinforces the existence of the something one wanted to diversify to begin with. In his book *On reason: Rationality in a world of cultural conflict and racism*, philosopher Emmanuel Eze (2008) sought a way out of this dilemma by focusing on the conditions that bring about acts of thought, rather than focusing on thinking itself. His conclusion supports the stance taken throughout this book: "Diversity constitutes a necessary condition of thinking in general. Without diversity there is no thought" (p. 3).

As argued throughout the book, each mode of thinking puts forward a particular image of thought as a way to understand and theorize a form of engagement with meaning. A curriculum, therefore, that hopes to foster thinking must be inclusive of a wide range of qualitative research traditions, interdisciplinary topics, and cultural voices (Preissle & deMarrais, 2011). In my teaching I try, whenever possible, to draw on a wide variety of disciplinary sources and include a culturally diverse group of scholars' work. Providing a diversity of perspectives accomplishes two things: First, it disrupts what Lorde (1984) calls a "mythical norm," and helps us develop our own critical reflexivity for how we inadvertently, or intentionally, participate in the construction of difference. A mythical norm is a norm against which we construct our identities, such as in the United States, being white, heterosexual, able-bodied, and so on. Lorde cautions, however, that "those of us who stand outside that power often identify one way in which we are different, and we assume that to be the primary cause of all oppression, forgetting other distortions around difference, some of which we ourselves may be practising" (p. 116). Using a wide range of research examples that demonstrate competing theories in practice promotes awareness of the strengths and limitations of different design decisions and the complex ethical issues embedded in all research. Second, and related, an inclusive curriculum contributes to the development of diversity by providing models for students who may not have been aware that their way of thinking and viewing the world was either valid, or practiced and taught by others. Providing a range of "whos" and "hows" from which to develop one's own thinking supports the point made in Chapter 1 that one needs exposure to diversity to imagine analysis differently. However, as I argue next, teaching for change raises the same issue dialectical thinking does for analysis; exposure to difference without some form of critical engagement is not enough. Without critical and reflexive engagement it is too easy to dismiss the other perspective without actually listening and attending to what that perspective has to say, and what it potentially can teach us about our own perspective and its position in the world we share. Elizabeth Chiseri-Strater (1996) explains: "to be reflective does not demand an 'other,' while to be reflexive demands both an other and some self-conscious awareness of the process of self-scrutiny" (p. 130, as quoted in Pillow, 2003, p. 177).

Since interpretation always opens up its inherent multiplicity, the hermeneutic task is not the outcome of the interpretive act, but developing a better understanding of the act of interpretation itself. It is vital, then, that we learn to work this critical space with our eyes wide open to its constraints, as well as its potentials. This is not a straightforward process and "involves the ability to *listen* for the subject matters that speak through the other's voice" (Davey, 2006, p. 69). In other words, understanding requires not only exposure to diverse perspectives, but the willingness to have our own understanding transformed in the process.

On Tradition

As demonstrated in Chapter 4 on dialectical thinking, dialecticians struggle with how to get out of what has often been called the *hermeneutic circle*. Originally, the hermeneutic circle was conceptualized as a way to account for the interpretation of a given text. An interpretation was considered legitimate when it showed how each part of a text was integrated into "a self-consistent unity of meaning and when . . . [it] also show[ed] how the whole of the meaning of the text contributes to the meaning of each of its parts" (Warnke, 2011, p. 94). However, as the histories of hermeneutics and of qualitative research demonstrate, that conceptualization of interpretation is no longer valid since any interpretive "circle" must also account for the presence and influence of the interpreter. Hans-Georg Gadamer's philosophical hermeneutics rearticulates the movement of understanding in a useful way. For Gadamer, understanding is conceptualized as "the interplay of the movement of tradition and the movement of the interpreter" (Gadamer, 1989, p. 293), where "tradition is recognized as a continuity of conflict, [and] as a process that conserves difficulty by passing on the questions that each age must confront in its own way" (Davey, 2006, pp. 163–4). In other words, "tradition is not simply a permanent precondition; rather, we produce it ourselves inasmuch as we understand, participate in the evolution of tradition, and hence further determine it ourselves" (Gadamer, 1989, p. 293).

All research, therefore, whether it does this consciously or not, is a participant in this interplay between tradition, the topic at hand, and its interpretation. Tradition is not an object of knowledge that exists outside of who we are, but always asserts itself in whatever we think and do. It is what prompts us to consider something to be significant as opposed to being something unworthy of our attention (Gadamer, 1989). As such, we must take seriously its effects on our thinking and doing. Since tradition is often defined as a fixed body of knowledge that must be transcended, this hermeneutic perspective can be a difficult one to take. However, I believe that understanding tradition as a particular form of participation in the continuation and transformation of a set of significant issues and subject matters (Davey, 2006) aligns well with a field such as qualitative research described as "a constantly shifting historical formation . . . embrac[ing] tensions and contradictions, including disputes over its methods and the forms its findings and interpretations take" (Denzin & Lincoln, 2011, p. 6).

Hermeneutical engagement supports the understanding of this "constantly shifting historical formation" because its purpose is "to clarify the conditions in which understanding takes place" (Gadamer, 1989, p. 295). These conditions, both past and present, are not always readily available to us, and often become concealed, or altered altogether, in the proliferation of new and innovative research designs and paradigms. So, on the one hand, the modes of thinking can be understood as resulting from paradigm shifts "triggered by problems that could not be resolved either by the field's standard operating research procedures or by its established ways of thinking" (Donmoyer, 2008, p. 591)—because each mode of thinking is not simply a new strategy developed within an established idea of qualitative research, but also alters how reality is constituted. On the other hand, as mentioned throughout this book, the boundaries formed around each mode of thinking are porous, and researchers do cross boundaries and carry out research in ways that combine two or more modes of thinking. In their chapter revisiting the paradigm debate, Yvonna Lincoln, Susan Lynham, and Egon Guba (2011) suggest that even the idea of a paradigm seems to be losing some of its argumentative leverage as paradigms are re-interpreted, mixed, and even found "to 'interbreed'" (p. 97). They conclude: "Consequently, to argue that it is paradigms that are in contention is probably less useful than to probe where and how paradigms exhibit confluence and where and how they exhibit differences, controversies, and contradictions" (p. 97). This requires a deeper understanding of these confluences and controversies.

Ultimately what I hope to achieve in my teaching is fostering awareness and understanding of the nature of learning itself, which I see as occurring when we engage openly and critically with the way tradition exerts its influence on the work researchers do. As participants in the meaning-making discourses of society, research is a hermeneutic act, and requires critical reflexivity. Although all modes of thinking have strengths and limitations resulting from their core characteristics, in many cases it is their uncritical use by uninformed or careless researchers that have resulted in some form of injustice to participants either in the study or through dissemination of the results. This is an important distinction because it suggests that an awareness of the core issues associated with particular strategies is a necessary part of reflexive research. Feminist scholar Wanda Pillow (2003) argues that reflexivity "not only contributes to producing knowledge that aids in understanding and gaining insight into the workings of our social world . . . [it] also provides insight on how this knowledge is produced" (p. 178). By demonstrating how the strategies we employ as researchers participate in the structures that give some knowledge legitimacy over other, researchers are better prepared to work with this complexity in ways that (hopefully) support the acknowledgment and legitimation of diverse ways of thinking and reasoning (Denzin & Lincoln, 2011; Eze, 2008). We cannot do this critical work outside of thinking, since, as educator Eduardo Duarte (2009) states, thinking is itself "the activity that counters the legitimation of existing forms of knowledge. . . . Thinking differently produces a difference *in* the world because thinking is itself an encounter *with* difference" (p. 250).

On Reflexive Dialogical Practice

Engagement can take many forms. Reflexive dialogue allows us to enter the movement of understanding and participate in making visible deep-seated, but often hidden, ongoing human concerns, as well as deep-seated and persistent structures that obscure the workings of oppression and dominance. But, as anyone who has read a difficult text would attest, understanding is best achieved when the theoretical is applied concretely to a topic of interest or problem needing to be addressed. Davey (2006) explains: "Application is not grasped as a mere carrying out of an order, as a dutiful application of a rule but as a knowing how to render for oneself what a text asks, a knowing how to translate into one's own terms what it asks of one" (p. 111).

The distinction made by management scholar Paula Jarzabkowski (2004) between "practice" and "practices" introduces this interaction between theory and practice well: "Practice is the actual activity, events, or work of strategy, while practices are those traditions, norms, rules, and routines through which the work of strategy is constructed" (p. 545). By combining critical dialogue about practices with hands-on practical experience with analysis, I aim for students to develop a deeper understanding of the interactions always occurring between practice and practices as these are taken up in diverse combinations as they inquire into issues they deem significant.

Teaching qualitative analysis provides a fertile place for reflexive engagement because analysis cannot be taught; it is something you need to engage in, encounter, negotiate, and try out. By applying the theories and methodologies learned not only do they begin to make sense, they also begin to lose their relativistic potential. No longer can one approach be considered as equally valid as another when the effects each produce are so drastically different. Analysis provides the space for reflexive thinking because the arguments put forward in the analytical process force a hermeneutic mediation between tradition, the data collected or generated, and the intended audience for the dissemination of results. It is here that novice researchers begin to feel the influence of intersecting traditions, and the implications of their chosen orientations on the discourse of power and knowledge. Furthermore, as novice researchers take on the analytical task, they begin to gain concrete understanding for three fundamental principles that I emphasize in my teaching: first, the need to do analysis to understand analysis; second, the importance of understanding the relationship between analysis and interpretation; and third, the essential role of writing.

1. *The need to do analysis to understand analysis.* One of the challenges of learning and teaching qualitative analysis is convincing novice researchers of the need to jump into the analytic work in order to determine what that work is going to involve. This seems counterintuitive, but we gain competence in most practices (for example, riding a bike, teaching a class, or learning a language) through practice, and practice involves trial and error, joy and frustration, and sometimes the need to go back to the drawing board and start again. An issue for novice researchers is how time-consuming this is, and they become concerned about wasting valuable time if what they are doing results in dead ends. In the context of higher education, where it seems more needs to be accomplished in less time, this is a real concern. Unfortunately, there are no shortcuts to the process of analysis and, more often than not, when these are attempted the result suffers. For this reason, I encourage students to spend time with their data, and require that they read whatever data set they are working with line-by-line. I encourage them to engage in this close reading, and question, annotate, name or code, chunk and identify what is there, without yet worrying what it might mean. I do this because the tendency for many is to leap into interpretation, to wonder why a statement was made, or an action was carried out, without really considering the range of statements and actions presented in the data and, conversely, those that are absent. In other words, the desire to interpret, to make sense of what something means, overshadows analysis or the careful study of the components of what is there.

This tendency is one I actively try to interrupt and I explain to students, even those who claim not to believe in coding (see St. Pierre (2011) for a compelling argument against coding), that the thinking enabled by coding as a process of taking stock of what is there, does not bind them to carry out their analysis in any predetermined way. Maggie MacLure (2013), although rejecting the notion of coding as a predefined process, argues that this dwelling is important, that a certain giving over of oneself to the process may open up unforeseen connections and potentials. As a result of taking this stance students have acknowledged, more often than not, that the process not only allowed them to see things in the data not previously noted as significant, but also to realize that, until pressed to do so, they were not actually reading or attending to the data, but glossing over it. This kind of reading is challenging because it pushes students into a form of interaction guided by their own intuitions and interests, which can be unsettling for students who often wonder whether they are going about it in the "right" way. To me this question indicates that they are thinking about what they are doing as they are doing it, and I remind them to take note of their decisions because these provide the foundation for principle number two.

2. *The importance of understanding the relationship between analysis and interpretation.* However frequently stated in introductory texts on qualitative research, the mantra "show, don't tell" or, as linguist Adrian Holliday (2007) calls it "showing the workings," is not easily adopted or understood by novice researchers. Novice researchers have particular difficulty in understanding that the analytical work they conduct creates the justification, provides the evidence for the interpretations that result from that work, and sets the stage for the organization and style of presentation for those interpretations. Furthermore, even when they do understand this relationship, they have trouble knowing how to show their procedures and decisions in a way that supports the presentation of the results—in whatever form they take or however understood. Complicating matters are concerns for what counts as "meaningful coherence" and "significant contribution" (Tracy, 2010) for qualitative research, and for social science research at large (Denzin, 2011). Not only is there no agreement for what constitutes quality research between these two broad areas, there is no agreement within the field of qualitative research itself (Denzin, 2011; Freeman, et al., 2007). This lack of agreed criteria generates much angst among students and novice scholars who, more often than not, are navigating and seeking to synthesize multiple, often competing discourses (for example, disciplinary, personal, theoretical, methodological, institutional, programmatic, and so on).

One of the challenges of introducing a range of theories for research is that each mode of thinking described in this book puts into practice particular ways of seeing and describing the nature of reality and truth, and as a result draws on different theoretical frameworks to do so. Rather than doing phenomenology or poststructuralism, I believe that attending to the interaction between theory and practice helps to better understand how you are putting the theory, for example phenomenology, to work analytically. Working from the strategies themselves develops the understanding that no two qualitative studies will be the same because each puts into play a unique set of data, circumstances, motivations, skills, and interests. Therefore, simply naming a study phenomenological is not sufficient. Furthermore, the diversity inherent to qualitative analysis inspires bricolage, suggesting that a better grasp of the differences between modes of thinking should help provide support for the arguments justifying the design decisions being made (Jarzabkowski, 2004). In other words, when theories and methodologies are mixed, they may emphasize some guiding assumptions over others or necessitate the creation of new rationales altogether.

Since any adaptation can significantly alter the theoretical underpinnings of the strategies adopted to begin with, taking note of decisions as they are occurring becomes an important part of the analytical process. Furthermore, the process of adaptation means that concerns over correct procedures or over validity cannot be resolved prior to the analytical work; the argument must be developed in the midst of this work itself.

3. *The essential role of writing.* Writing, like analysis, is made up of false starts, careful thinking, narrow and broad wanderings, and untraceable leaps of imagination. There is no right way to go about doing it and no guides for when to end. There are plenty of examples to ponder and draw from, but in the end each study takes on its own direction and shape. A challenge for students and novice researchers is taking seriously the role that writing plays for thinking analytically. Phenomenologist Max van Manen explains:

> It is in the act of reading and writing that insights emerge. . . . It is precisely in the process of writing that the data of the research are gained as well as interpreted and that the fundamental nature of the research questions is perceived.
>
> *van Manen, 2006, p. 715*

Writing is itself a skill that is learned best when practiced, but, unfortunately, many of the conventions learned in educational contexts work against the kind of writing qualitative analysis encourages (Ely et al., 1997). Luckily most introductory texts on qualitative research emphasize the importance of writing (e.g., Holliday, 2007; Maxwell, 2013), and many texts provide a variety of orientations towards writing as a way to disrupt the perceived artificial separation of literary and scientific writing (for example, Clifford & Marcus, 1986; Richardson & St. Pierre, 2005), a separation that has long been repudiated in the field of qualitative research.

Writing serves analysis in multiple ways. It is "thinking on paper" (Maxwell, 2013, p. 20). For example, writing reflective or analytic "memos about our codes and comparisons and any other ideas about our data that occur to us" (Charmaz, 2014, p. 4) is a crucial part of analysis since it pushes us to articulate insights we are having in the moment; insights that may otherwise get lost. In addition, exposure to a variety of ways in which research is written about, and written up, helps students to understand that "by writing in different ways, we discover new aspects of our topic and our relationship to it" (Richardson, 2000, p. 923). Finally, arguing against writing as a writing of something else (that is, data or a representation of findings), St. Pierre (in Richardson & St. Pierre, 2005) views writing as "nomadic inquiry . . . [because] writing is thinking, writing is analysis, writing is indeed a seductive and tangled method of discovery" (p. 967). In other words, writing produces knowledge, meanings, provocations, rather than representing these things.

Regardless of the perspective taken on writing, and regardless of being told repeatedly to start writing early, even "before actually engaging in fieldwork" (Wolcott, 1994, p. 405), students and novice researchers have a difficult time embracing this practice. Part of the reason is due to the time it takes to put ideas onto paper, and part of it is apprehension and worry about committing to paper tentative or "fuzzy" ideas, under-thought claims, or misinterpretations. Writing continuously throughout the process of analysis, and writing in a variety of ways is one way in which students become more comfortable with the uncertainties of the research process.

Finally, writing is an important part of reflexivity and awareness of the role scholarly writing plays in the production of discourses about people (Smith, 1999). Just as there is no neutral analytical approach, there is no neutral writing style, and writing, like analysis, puts into practice ways of thinking about the world and its people. In fact, Holliday (2007) suggests that qualitative researchers think of themselves as writers, since "the very act of interpretation within qualitative research is itself integrated with the act of writing" (p. 15). Furthermore, he argues that all writing "is a product of a discourse community which cannot avoid ideology" (p. 15), so research writing needs to be as transparent as possible within the ideological commitments made by the researcher. A better understanding of this interaction is necessary, therefore, as you find your location in the broad range of analytical procedures available to you.

None of the activities described here are novel, but they do require a belief that time spent engaging, thinking, reflecting, processing, discussing, and playing with one's data is worthwhile. Like most instructors who incorporate a lot of hands-on activities in teaching, using class time productively is a source of worry, especially if students feel uncertain about the process, stare blankly into space, or panic about wasting time and needing to start all over again. However, I believe the resulting discomfort is worthwhile and, in many ways, part of the process for fostering an environment for reflexive dialogical practice since it pushes all of us, myself included, to better articulate our stances on different aspects of the research process. Furthermore, I believe this kind of environment is especially important to instill in introductory research courses because, as sociologist Zygmunt Bauman explains, the task of the researcher in these postmodern times characterized by pluralism, uncertainty, and the rejection of shared norms is undergoing dramatic change:

> To be effectively and consequentially present in a postmodern habitat sociology must conceive of itself as a participant . . . of this never ending, self-reflexive process of reinterpretation and devise its strategy accordingly. In practice, this will mean in all probability, replacing the ambitions of a judge of 'common beliefs', healer of prejudices and umpire of truth with those of a clarifier of interpretative rules and facilitator of

communication; this will amount to the replacement of the dream of the legislator with the practice of the interpreter.

Bauman, 1992, p. 204

Therefore, it seems more important than ever to gain a better understanding of how these multiple strategies are being taken up, interpreted, reorganized, merged, transformed, or disguised in everyday practice, including the institutional and disciplinary practices of inquiry. Teaching for diversity through reflexive dialogue and practice provides a space for qualitative researchers to try out, understand, interrogate, disrupt, rethink, and re-entangle the paradigmatic diversity while simultaneously re-creating what is understood as individuals, society, language, concepts, and the world.

Final Thoughts

Writing this book was more challenging than I expected. One of the challenges I experienced was figuring out how to draw from the theoretical and methodological literature to support my descriptions of the modes of thinking without simply reproducing one representative version. Furthermore, since the modes of thinking are meant to be abstractions of the range of uses and assumptions circulating in the literature, I needed to be mindful of my sources, seeking both to draw from diverse interdisciplinary conceptualizations, while also keeping a clear focus on those characteristics that I saw emerging from this diversity. I often found myself getting lost in the myriad ways terms like category, narrative, dialectics, poetics, and diagrams were being used by qualitative researchers, and found that qualitative research is indeed a messy field where "endless numbers of innovative ways to blend or transcend art and science in qualitative collection of empirical materials, analysis, and representation exist" (Ellingson, 2011, p. 600). As a result I wondered at times how useful the abstractions I was providing were going to be. And yet, at the same time, I began to see that not only was there a consistency across history in how these terms were being used, but this consistency transcended disciplines, taking shape in the arts as well as the sciences. This interdisciplinary consistency gave me encouragement to continue and find ways to sort through the literature and make tough decisions about how much to include in each of my portrayals.

As someone whose study of interpretation has been largely influenced by philosophical hermeneutics, I believe that understanding is brought forth in dialogical engagement with the diverse traditions that give shape to thinking. Whether our overall purpose is to conduct a quality interpretive study or extend our methodological designs beyond the imaginable, understanding the limitations and potentials of these traditions seems essential. Furthermore, I believe this book offers a way of assessing how these strategies have been employed in analytical approaches in particular disciplines and the nature of the conflicts that have arisen between them. As I studied the literature, I was particularly impressed with the key role dialectical thinking has played across the disciplines, moving various fields (including qualitative research) beyond categorical and narrative thinking to engage head on in debates about the role of research, language, values, ideology, and so on. Furthermore, developing a better understanding of the role certain approaches, such as Foucault's genealogy, played in these developments fueled my interest for the modes of thinking that did not seem to belong easily under any one mode of thinking, but participated rather in the paradigmatic shift occurring between modes. As a result, I am most critical of the information provided in the end-of-chapter sections on the strengths and limitations of the mode of thinking in question, since the content presented in these sections could have been better developed to tell a more coherent narrative of change. Overall, however, I feel satisfied that the descriptions offered here will serve the field of qualitative research and provide fertile material for the teaching and learning of qualitative data analysis.

Note

1 See Abend (2008), or Schwandt (1993), for interesting perspectives on the meaning and role of theory in the social sciences.

References

Abend, G. (2008). The meaning of 'theory.' *Sociological Theory, 26*(2), 173–99.

Bauman, Z. (1992). *Intimations of postmodernity.* New York, NY: Routledge.

Charmaz, K. (2014). *Constructing grounded theory* (2nd edn.). Thousand Oaks, CA: Sage.

Clifford, J., & Marcus, G. E. (Eds.). (1986). *Writing culture: The poetics and politics of ethnography.* Berkeley, CA: University of California Press.

Colebrook, C. (2002). *Gilles Deleuze.* London, UK: Routledge.

Coole, D., & Frost, S. (2010). 'Introducing the new materialisms.' In D. Coole and S. Frost (Eds.), *New materialisms: Ontology, agency, and politics* (pp. 1–43). Durham, NC: Duke University Press.

Davey, N. (2006). *Unquiet understanding: Gadamer's philosophical hermeneutics.* Albany, NY: State University of New York Press.

De Certeau, M. (1984). *The practice of everyday life.* Berkeley, CA: University of California Press.

Denzin, N. K. (2011). 'The politics of evidence.' In N. K. Denzin & Y. S. Lincoln (Eds.), *The Sage handbook of qualitative research* (4th edn., pp. 645–57). Thousand Oaks, CA: Sage.

Denzin, N. K., & Lincoln, Y. S. (2011). 'Introduction: The discipline and practice of qualitative research.' In N. K. Denzin & Y. S. Lincoln (Eds.), *The Sage handbook of qualitative research* (4th edn., pp. 1–19). Thousand Oaks, CA: Sage.

Donmoyer, R. (2008). 'Paradigm.' In L. M. Given (Ed.), *The Sage encyclopedia of qualitative research methods* (Vol. 2, pp. 591–5). Thousand Oaks, CA: Sage.

Duarte, E. M. (2009). In the time of thinking differently. *Philosophy of Education Yearbook,* 250–2.

Ellingson, L. L. (2011). 'Analysis and representation across the continuum.' In N. K. Denzin & Y. S. Lincoln (Eds.), *The Sage handbook of qualitative research* (4th edn., pp. 595–610). Thousand Oaks, CA: Sage.

Ely, M., Vinz, R., Downing, M., & Anzul, M. (1997). *On writing qualitative research: Living by words*. Bristol, PA: The Falmer Press.

Erickson, F. (2011). 'A history of qualitative inquiry in social and educational research.' In N. K. Denzin & Y. S. Lincoln (Eds.), *The Sage handbook of qualitative research* (4th edn., pp. 43–59). Thousand Oaks, CA: Sage.

Eze, E. C. (2008). *On reason: Rationality in a world of cultural conflict and racism*. Durham, NC: Duke University Press.

Foucault, M. (1970). *The order of things: An archaeology of human sciences*. New York, NY: Random House.

Freedman, L. (2013). *Strategy: A history*. New York, NY: Oxford University Press.

Freeman, M., deMarrais, K., Preissle, J., Roulston, K., & St. Pierre, E. A. (2007). Standards of evidence in qualitative research: An incitement to discourse. *Educational Researcher, 36*(1), 25–32.

Gadamer, H.-G. (1989). *Truth and method* (2nd revised edn., trans. by J. Weinsheimer & D. G. Marshall). New York: Continuum (original work published 1975).

Greene, J. C., & Hall, J. N. (2010). 'Dialectics and pragmatism: Being of consequence.' In A. Tashakkori & C. Teddlie (Eds.), *Handbook of mixed methods in social and behavioral research* (pp. 119–44). Thousand Oaks, CA: Sage.

Holliday, A. (2007). *Doing and writing qualitative research* (2nd edn.). London: Sage.

Jarzabkowski, P. (2004). Strategy as practice: Recursiveness, adaptation, and practices-in-use. *Organization Studies, 25*(4), 529–60.

Kincheloe, J. L. (2001). Describing the bricolage: Conceptualizing a new rigor in qualitative research. *Qualitative Inquiry, 7*(6), 679–92.

Lather, P. (2006). Paradigm proliferation as a good thing to think with: Teaching research in education as a wild profusion. *International Journal of Qualitative Studies in Education, 19*(1), 35–57.

Lincoln, Y. S., Lynham, S. A., & Guba, E. G. (2011). 'Paradigmatic controversies, contradictions, and emerging confluences, revisited.' In N. K. Denzin & Y. S. Lincoln (Eds.), *The Sage handbook of qualitative research* (4th edn., pp. 97–128). Thousand Oaks, CA: Sage.

Lorde, A. (1984). *Sister outsider: Essays and speeches*. Freedom, CA: Crossing Press.

MacLure, M. (2013). 'Classification or wonder? Coding as an analytic practice in qualitative research.' In R. Coleman & J. Ringrose (Eds.), *Deleuze and research methodologies* (pp. 164–83). Edinburgh, UK: Edinburgh University Press.

Maxwell, J. A. (2013). *Qualitative research design: An interactive approach* (3rd edn.). Thousand Oaks, CA: Sage.

Palmer, R. E. (1980). The liminality of Hermes and the meaning of hermeneutics. *Proceedings of the Heraclitean Society: A Quarterly Report on Philosophy and Criticism of the Arts and Sciences* (Michigan State University, Kalamazoo), *5*, 4–11.

Pillow, W. S. (2003). Confession, catharsis, or cure? Rethinking the uses of reflexivity as methodological power in qualitative research. *International Journal of Qualitative Studies in Education, 16*(2), 175–96.

Prasad, P. (2005). *Crafting qualitative research: Working in the postpositivist traditions*. Armonk, NY: M. E. Sharpe, Inc.

Preissle, J. (2011). 'Qualitative futures: Where we might go from where we've been.' In N. K. Denzin & Y. S. Lincoln (Eds.), *The Sage handbook of qualitative research* (4th edn., pp. 685–98). Thousand Oaks, CA: Sage.

Preissle, J., & deMarrais, K. (2011). 'Teaching qualitative research responsively.' In N. K. Denzin & M. D. Giardina (Eds.), *Qualitative inquiry and global crises* (pp. 31–9). Walnut Creek, CA: Left Coast Press.

Richardson, L. (2000). 'Writing: A method of inquiry.' In N. K. Denzin & Y. S. Lincoln (Eds.), *Handbook of qualitative research* (2nd edn., pp. 923–48). Thousand Oaks, CA: Sage.

Richardson, L., & St. Pierre, E. A. (2005). 'Writing: A method of inquiry.' In N. K. Denzin & Y. S. Lincoln (Eds.), *The Sage handbook of qualitative research* (3rd edn., pp. 959–78). Thousand Oaks, CA: Sage.

Schwandt, T. A. (1993). 'Theory for the moral sciences: Crisis of identity and purpose.' In G. Mills & D. J. Flinders (Eds.), *Theory and concepts in qualitative research* (pp. 5–23). New York, NY: Teachers College Press.

Smith, L. T. (1999). *Decolonizing methodologies: Research and indigenous peoples.* London, UK: Zed Books.

St. Pierre, E. A. (2011). 'Post qualitative research: The critique and the coming after.' In N. K. Denzin & Y. S. Lincoln (Eds.), *The Sage handbook of qualitative research* (4th edn., pp. 611–25). Thousand Oaks, CA: Sage.

Tracy, S. J. (2010). Qualitative quality: Eight "big-tent" criteria for excellent qualitative research. *Qualitative Inquiry, 16*(10), 837–51.

van Manen, M. (2006). Writing qualitatively, or the demands of writing. *Qualitative Health Research, 16*(5), 713–22.

Warnke, G. (2011). The hermeneutic circle versus dialogue. *The Review of Metaphysics, 65*(1), 91–112.

Wolcott, H. F. (1994). *Transforming qualitative data: Description, analysis, and interpretation.* Thousand Oaks, CA: Sage.

INDEX

Taylor & Francis eBooks

Helping you to choose the right eBooks for your Library

Add Routledge titles to your library's digital collection today. Taylor and Francis ebooks contains over 50,000 titles in the Humanities, Social Sciences, Behavioural Sciences, Built Environment and Law.

Choose from a range of subject packages or create your own!

Benefits for you
- » Free MARC records
- » COUNTER-compliant usage statistics
- » Flexible purchase and pricing options
- » All titles DRM-free.

REQUEST YOUR **FREE** INSTITUTIONAL TRIAL TODAY

Free Trials Available
We offer free trials to qualifying academic, corporate and government customers.

Benefits for your user
- » Off-site, anytime access via Athens or referring URL
- » Print or copy pages or chapters
- » Full content search
- » Bookmark, highlight and annotate text
- » Access to thousands of pages of quality research at the click of a button.

eCollections – Choose from over 30 subject eCollections, including:

Archaeology	Language Learning
Architecture	Law
Asian Studies	Literature
Business & Management	Media & Communication
Classical Studies	Middle East Studies
Construction	Music
Creative & Media Arts	Philosophy
Criminology & Criminal Justice	Planning
Economics	Politics
Education	Psychology & Mental Health
Energy	Religion
Engineering	Security
English Language & Linguistics	Social Work
Environment & Sustainability	Sociology
Geography	Sport
Health Studies	Theatre & Performance
History	Tourism, Hospitality & Events

For more information, pricing enquiries or to order a free trial, please contact your local sales team:
www.tandfebooks.com/page/sales

 Routledge
Taylor & Francis Group | The home of Routledge books

www.tandfebooks.com